A Life on Purpose

WISDOM AT WORK

Therese!

May "A Life..." reveal how pregnefecant we are as MIRACLE workers — bring your miracles to the world.

Joan C King
6/20/13

Also by Joan C. King

Cellular Wisdom for Women: An Inner Work Book

The Code of Authentic Living: Cellular Wisdom

A Life on Purpose

WISDOM AT WORK

JOAN C. KING

Fort Collins, Colorado

Cover Design: Teresa Espaniola
Interior Design: 1106 Design

Library of Congress Cataloging-in-Publication Data   2012914553
King, Joan C.
A life on purpose: wisdom at work/Joan C. King
Includes bibliographical references.

ISBN-13: 978-0-9859860-0-1

1. Personal growth, life situations, career, work 2. Self-Improvement through work aligned with self-awareness 3. Creative Problem Solving life skills in category of work, spiritual guidance 4. Self-actualization (Psychology) (Spirituality), etc. 5. Inspiration Heart-warming life purpose stories of overcoming to success 6. Purpose in category of work, career, finding one's purpose in life 7. Body's wisdom (Principles of Biology and Physiology)—how the body's wisdom mirrors the wisdom of our larger lives, models, and principles, etc.

I. Title

Manufactured in the United States of America

Self Published.

10 9 8 7 6 5 4 3 2 1

Dedication

To the hosts of courageous individuals who have forged a new path to create personal success and make their valuable contributions to the world. Thank You!

To the readers of this book who will forge their unique paths, we need your contributions to make the world whole!

Author's Note

Cellular Wisdom™ reveals how fundamental truths for living an authentic, fulfilling life are coded in the elegantly complex dance of chemical and energetic interactions within and between our cells. Just as a single human cell is orchestrated from a nucleus at its center, for example, an individual must live life from their core essence to be healthy and whole. Only when cells connect with other cells do they fulfill their potential; in the same spirit, we achieve our grandest purposes in relationship with others. Over thousands of years of evolution, the human body has identified principles such as moderation, diversity, and compassion as essential to its survival. When we learn to appreciate and apply these same principles to our everyday lives, we learn to live a more balanced, focused, exuberant life. Cellular Wisdom™ shows us how to interpret the truths that our bodies teach and how to apply them to our physical, mental, emotional-social, and spiritual lives.

Table of Contents

1

A New Story

*One thing I know: the only ones among you who will be really
happy are those who will have sought and found how to serve.*

—ALBERT SCHWEITZER

Between Stories

We live in a **world in crisis.** We are faced with a crisis of security. The real estate and banking systems are in turmoil. Workers are being laid off in alarming numbers. People still on the job wonder if they will be next as they attempt to juggle their jobs as well as the jobs of those no longer employed. Those laid off are uncertain that they will find employment in a shrinking job market. We are faced with a crisis of identity, of values, and of our relationship with our innermost being. We don't know who we are or what is most important in life. We are left without a compass by which to navigate. Without knowing who we are or what is most important, we are not able to align with our inner highest self. We face a poverty and crisis of integrity. There is a crisis of leadership, a woeful lack of authentic leaders who are guided by their own integrity and alignment and who inspire integrity and alignment in those around them. Lack of energy, enthusiasm, joy, and a sense of purpose are the norm for those who are fortunate enough to have jobs, arising from an epidemic crisis of meaning.

How do individuals experience meaning in work? In a recent study[1] Laura Frey Horn concluded that transcendent individuals (i.e. those who continue to develop as adults into greater complexity) experience meaning in work as integral to their lives. She found that they are "often pioneers creating new meaning and new skills for self and others." Further, she found that if necessary, "they will leave an organization, usually to begin one that honors their fully integrated lives."

Alan Fricker describes our society as in ". . . crisis—ecological, social, economic crisis—because we do not have a good story.[2] **We are between stories.** The old story of how we understand the world . . . and how we fit into it is no longer effective. We have yet to learn the new story . . . ."

I believe the same crisis of meaning occurs in our individual lives as in society as a whole. It occurs when the old story no longer provides meaning for us. As Fricker describes, "We become alienated from our innermost selves but are unable to fully repress the hunger for meaning."

Stories

Chris Langan's Story

Chris Langan may be the smartest man in the world. His IQ is estimated at 195, which exceeds that of Einstein at 150. Chris began to speak at six months of age. He taught himself to read at three years, and questioned his father about the existence of God at five years of age. It would amaze everyone when he would show up at school for the exams and ace them when he did not attend classes.

---

[1] Horn, Laura Frey. 2006. The Experience of Meaning in Work for Transcendent Adults: A Phenomenological Study of Individuals at Spiral Dynamics integral (SDi) Theory Second-Tier Levels of Development. Ed.D., The George Washington University

[2] Fricker, Alan. 2001. The Hunger for Meaning. *Futures* 33, no. 2:171–180.

It seemed Chris Langan could have the world on his plate, reports Malcom Gladwell, author of *The Tipping Point* and *Blink* (Back Bay Books, 2002) and *Outliers: The Story of Success* (Little, Brown and Company, 2008).

Chris grew up in a home dominated by an angry, drunken step father in Bozeman, Montana. He describes his family as severely poor. He had no matched socks. His shoes had holes in them. His pants had holes in them. He had only one set of clothes. When Chris got a perfect score on the SAT and received a scholarship to attend Reed College in Portland, Oregon, it seemed his life was about to turn around.

Soon after Chris arrived, however, his troubles began. His classmates, whom he described as "long-haired city kids," felt foreign to this crew-cut Montana ranch hand. Then he lost his scholarship. Chris learned that his mother had failed to fill out some required financial statement paperwork in the specified period of time. What was his response? Amazingly, in spite of his desperate need for the scholarship, Chris made no attempt to explain what happened. He did not know what to say or to whom to say it. Even with his remarkable intelligence, Chris was unable to explain his problem and enlist someone to help him. Chris left Reed before finals and received "Fs" in all his classes. His error was to be compounded.

Later, Chris attempted to finish college closer to home at Montana State University. Once again, problems ensued. When the transmission fell out of his car, Chris did not have the money to get it repaired. The only way he could get to the university was to hitch a ride with a neighbor. Since the neighbor was unable to leave home before 11 a.m., Chris could not attend morning classes. Upon requesting a schedule that included only afternoon classes, Chris received this response from his advisor, ". . . after looking at your transcript at Reed College, I see that you have yet to learn that everyone has to make sacrifices to get an education. Request denied."

Chris abandoned any attempts to continue his higher education. Instead, he went on to take various jobs working in construction and on a clam boat in Long Island.

Eventually, Chris married. He now lives on a horse farm in Missouri and leads what he terms a double life strategy. In an interview with Esquire magazine writer Mike Sager, Chris describes his life: "You go to work, you do your job, you exchange pleasantries. On the other side, you come home and you begin doing equations in your head. You kind of retreat into your own world—you make it work for you the best you can." Chris continues to read and was fascinated by the work of Noam Chomsky, the linguist. He continues to write. For decades he has worked on his Cognition-Theoretic Model of the Universe (CTMU), described by Chris as a "Theory of Everything." In an interview with KMBC's Maria Antonia, Chris describes his theory as ". . . mapping a correspondence between language of thought and the real world." Yet, Chris has not yet found a publisher. He and his wife, Gina, have founded a non-profit corporation called the Mega Foundation to "create and implement programs that aid in the development of severely gifted individuals and their ideas." *http://www.megafoundation.org/NOEON/Articles/Academia.html*

Chris's abusive and suppressive background coupled with his academic failure crippled him. His resentment of authority prevented him from learning to stand up for himself and request what he really wanted. The smartest man in the world told KMBC's Maria Antonia, "I'm at peace with myself. I actually enjoy my life. We have a lovely place here."

Message to the Reader

Chris had an opportunity to escape his "poverty of spirit" at Reed College. What if he had explained himself, his circumstances, his desires, and his needs? Would Chris's advisor at Reed College have given him an opportunity to regain his scholarship if he had explained his mother's error and had asked for what he wanted? What if Chris had explained his situation to the advisor at Montana State or had found someone to speak on his behalf? We cannot know the answers to these questions.

What we can know is that Chris's contribution to the world is marginalized. His influence, which could have extended broadly, is minimized. If he had received the training he needed, Chris could possibly today be interacting with a broad array of graduate students and faculty, teaching and influencing others to think more deeply. Although extraordinarily intelligent beyond a measurement, Chris lacked knowledge of how the world works and lacked training in navigating its ways. He lacked experience to know that he might have spoken up on his own behalf. And he most certainly lacked the tools needed for pursuing dreams. His background failed to give him these. You see, smart as he was, Chris didn't know what he didn't know. He didn't know how to assess both his obvious strengths and how important his contribution might be to the world, and his weaknesses and how to make a plan that would help compensate for them. He didn't have a plan of action. He didn't know how to navigate around obstacles once they appeared before him or how to take smart risks. He didn't know how or when to ask for advice or help. He didn't know how to avail himself of his own inner resources, and instead of doors opening for him, they shut in his face. As a result, tragically, the world has been robbed of the brilliant contributions Chris was capable of offering, and Chris has been robbed of the joy and satisfaction of making them. Yes, Chris is making a contribution through his foundation, but neither he nor the world will ever know what astounding discoveries might have been possible.

The system as it is failed Chris Langan. This is a clear example of how the old ways of doing things are no longer working, because as was suggested above, we are between stories. Normal people like you and me must not just learn the new story, but to begin to write it. A few are already on their way. We will attempt to point out what they are doing that is different and how it is different. The principles and benefits presented in this book are available to all who have an inner yearning for something more and the courage to reach for it. If you ache for something you might not be able to define, this may be the book you've been waiting for.

I would hope that the first ingredient in the new story would be wisdom, a quality that seems slippery to define and even more slippery to employ. Leadership researchers recognize wisdom as an integral component for a new story: "A better future is possible if we are able to look beyond the accumulative assumptions about knowledge (and technology) to wisdom. Wisdom is a way of being and is fundamentally practical in a complex and uncertain world."[3]

Wisdom integrates unconscious and conscious ways of knowing. Wisdom is characterized by a deep insight into people, things, events or situations. Tapping into wisdom we optimally (effectively and efficiently) apply perceptions and knowledge to produce desired results. Wisdom allows us to recognize what is true or right and couple that with optimum judgment leading to action.

Here is a working definition for the purposes of our inquiry together. Let's lay aside our previous conceptions of what wisdom means—since we are creating a new story.

Where does one turn for wisdom in investigating, exploring, and filling this inner yearning? Where can one go for guidance? The new story cannot be the regurgitation or rehash of principles and methodologies past. So, where can one look for inspiration?

I have experienced the inexpressible yearning to find wisdom. As a scientist, I studied cells and their behavior. I was repeatedly awed by the inherent intelligence and wisdom expressed in the body as it seeks to grow, mature, reproduce, and operate optimally in concert with other cells in the body. Could it be that the wisdom inherent in the cells might offer guidance in my search for meaning? This was out-of-the-box thinking for a science professor, but I decided to follow my yearning. My story will be told as these chapters unfold—how I moved from uncertainty and yearning into a career that not only fills me full, but that also propels me along in my own evolution, a career that expresses my purpose.

What is Purpose and How Does One Live on It?

What is meant by "purpose?" What is "Life on Purpose?" These are tricky questions to answer definitively. For the sake of our discussion and of writing a new story, I will focus on the meaning available to me today.

---

[3] Paul B. Baltes and Ursula M. Staudinger. Wisdom: A metaheuristic (pragmatic) to orchestrate mind and virtue toward excellence. *American Psychologist* 55 (1):122–136, 2000.

Your Purpose is your expression of your innermost being in the outer world. It is how you choose to make your own contribution. It is integral to the element of "work" in your life.

There is a significant difference between rattling through life, reacting to circumstances as you go like a pinball machine on one hand, and choosing your life course with volition and determination on the other. This is a deeper level of the meaning of Purpose. It is well worth pursuing. There are many who are already on their way. Maybe you are one of them. Finding this empowerment is one of the first rungs on our ladder of the evolutionary path. (To distinguish this deeper meaning from the everyday meaning, we will use a capital P when referring to the deeper and larger Purpose.)

Purpose is about expressing our unique gifts in the outer world through our work, our relationships, our recreation, and our service to self and others. It is about our relationship with the rest of the world.

The evidence of this appears in the stories you will encounter in these pages. We are beginning to turn to the next rung or evolutionary step: choosing to discover our Purpose, our highest calling, our greatest contribution to the world, utilizing our deepest inner resources and an integration of all our life skills and abilities. This is the preference of our essential being.

When you travel on this path doors open, synchronicities may occur, and you perhaps find yourself somewhere you had never dreamed in your wildest imagining. It's all good. This path is like being in love, where you are likely to go around with a silly grin on your face wondering, "Why me? Why did I get so lucky?" It's like walking through a doorway to find yourself sucked into a vortex of infinite possibilities and their fulfillment—similar to Alice arriving in Wonderland, except this is no fairy tale. Purpose taps into the incredible creative power at the core of our being. That is precisely what we want to explore in these pages because therein lies our greatness.

This journey is available to anyone with the openness to learn and the will and courage to choose their way. You might think you don't have these qualities. Don't be fooled. If that is what you think, you have not yet discovered who you are; but you can. The journey is inside, not "out there" somewhere.

Richard Leider publishes a journal about taking charge of your work/life, "On Purpose." He tells us: "Purpose is the anchor that secures us to life, which anchors us during crisis, which keeps us going when nothing else does. It fits things together. It gives meaning in times of uncertainty or loss."

"It's not about asking what is the meaning of life, but rather asking what your life means. It's being willing to receive the truth of what you hear."

Dawna Markova, a psychotherapist and CEO of Professional Thinking Partners, Inc., consultants whose expertise lies in the expansion of human capacity, writes, "In West Africa, there is a saying that it's the heart that lets go and the hands that follow." I'm coming to understand that there is no such thing as finding one's purpose. It's about creating the conditions, for six months or six minutes, where your purpose can find you, from her book, *I Will Not Die an Unlived Life: Reclaiming Purpose and Passion* (Conari Press, 2000).

Stories

Greg Mortenson's Story

Greg Mortenson, author of *Three Cups of Tea* and *Stones into Schools* (Penguin Books, 2007), found his Life's Purpose in a tiny village in northern Pakistan at the feet of K2, the world's second highest peak in the Karakoram mountain range of the Himalayas, even though he did not go there in search of it.

As a young man in his mid-thirties and bouncing between inconsequential jobs, Mortenson made an attempt in 1993 to climb K2 in honor of his younger sister, Christa, recently deceased from a massive seizure after a lifelong struggle with epilepsy. Growing up on the slopes of Mt. Kilimanjaro, the son of the founders of Kilimanjaro Christian Medical Center and the International School Moshi, Greg's plan was to lay an amber necklace that had been his sister's, wrapped in a Tibetan prayer flag, on the rocks at the summit of K2. Due to an emergency rescue required by another climber, Mortenson did not reach the summit, and on his descent got separated from his guide and other members of his climbing team. After days of wandering at high altitude without food and very little water, he stumbled upon the village of Korphe, miles away from the meeting place of his porters and fellow climbers, where he was nurtured back to health by the remote but generous villagers. Mortenson came to know these villagers intimately during his period of recuperation and learned a great deal about their values and culture. One day Greg encountered a group of village children sitting on the bare ground writing with sticks in the dirt to perform their lessons. Moved both by the care given him by the villagers and by the poverty of their circumstance, Mortenson promised village elders to help them build a school.

When he returned to his home in California, Greg found that gaining support and funding to fulfill his rash, though heartfelt, promise was not as easy as he had hoped. In his own words, "When I came back to the States, I wrote 580 letters to celebrities, businessmen, and other prominent Americans soliciting donations for my school project in Pakistan. The only reply I got was from Tom Brokaw who wrote a check for $100. I submitted sixteen grant proposals and they were all rejected. Then I sold my possessions, my car and climbing gears, cleaned out my savings account and cashed in my University of California retirement policy where I had worked as a trauma nurse. All in all I raised only $2,000. I spoke to a group of elementary school children in River Falls, Wisconsin, where my mom was the principal. The school children were sympathetic to the kids without a school in Pakistan. They went to their piggy banks and donated 64,000 pennies. Then Dr. Jean Hoerni, a Swiss climber and microchip physicist sent $12,000 to build my school. Dr. Hoerni also convinced Arthur Rock, a venture capitalist to support my efforts. Before I could build my school, the Korphe villagers told me they need a 282-foot suspension bridge over a frothing river to transport building materials for the school. In 1995 the bridge was built in ten weeks. When the time came to build the school, a village elder picked up wooden planks and carried them on his back. The planks weighed about 100 pounds, yet this elder who reads the Koran to the villagers was the first to pitch in and help. The local villagers had tears in their eyes when they saw this, and they all volunteered to help." The school was built as promised.

News spread and requests for more schools poured in and one thing led to another. Greg co-founded with Dr. Hoerni the Central Asia Institute, a nonprofit organization for funding and managing the various projects, and went on the road soliciting funds for building more schools and paying teachers. Soon he co-authored the bestselling book, *Three Cups of Tea* (Penguin, 2007), the title of which came from the villagers' tale of the Balti proverb: "The first time you share tea with a Balti, you are a stranger. The second time you take tea, you are an honored guest. The third time you share a cup of tea, you become family." Mortenson shared many cups of tea during the months of his recuperation, and more than that, he was one Westerner who kept his promise. The village elders became his friends and family in Pakistan for life.

Mortenson certainly faced his share of challenges. He was kidnapped by the Taliban in Pakistan and survived eight days of confinement in 1996. In 2003, he hid for eight hours under decaying animal hides in the back of a truck to escape a firefight between feuding warlords. He has overcome two fatwehs, rulings from Islamic law, from Islamic mullahs angered by his education of girls. He has been investigated by the CIA for working in remote and volatile regions of Afghanistan and Pakistan. He's received hate mail and death threats following 9/11 from American citizens for his work helping to educate Muslim children.

Greg insisted that his publisher change the subtitle of *Three Cups of Tea* "One Man's Mission to Fight Terrorism One School at a Time" to "One Man's Mission to Promote Peace . . . One School at a Time," and eventually succeeded. His position was, "If you fight terrorism, it's based in fear. If you promote peace, it's based in hope." Interestingly, once the change was accepted by the publisher, sales soared. Mortenson believes that the surest way to social and economic change—and peace—is through educating the upcoming generations, particularly the girls.

Says the Central Asia Institute website, *www.ikat.org,* "The tribal communities of northern Pakistan taught Mortenson a critical lesson in our first five years of existence: sustainable and successful development can only occur when projects are entirely initiated, implemented, and managed by local communities. It is also important to listen and learn from the local communities served, rather than impose external evaluations or judgment of what is best from an outsider's perspective. The philosophy to empower the local people through their own initiative is at the heart of all CAI programs . . . A few additional projects have been introduced in Mongolia (rural health education) and Kyrgyzstan (teacher training scholarships). Over the first decade of CAI's evolution, our programs and projects expanded to several regions of Pakistan and Afghanistan with an emphasis on education, health issues, environment and cultural preservation." As of 2010, Mortenson has established over 145 schools in rural and often volatile regions of Pakistan and Afghanistan, which provide education to over 64,000 children, including 52,000 girls, where few education opportunities existed before.

This one man, Greg Mortenson, has found a way to introduce and support social and economic change in an extremely volatile part of the world. He hopes to "promote peace, one school at a time." He has received more awards and commendations than can be listed here. His thoughts on working with Afghan and northern Pakistani tribal leaders and local customs and values are sought, and taught, by US military commanders in Afghanistan. *Three Cups of Tea* is required reading for US Army special forces in the Middle East. He made a promise and kept it. He found his Life's Purpose, a single man ultimately making an important impact on the world in which we live.

Message to the Reader

When we examine Greg Mortenson's story, we find clues to the characteristics that distinguish Living on Purpose. Greg developed a dream as well as a vision of it being realized. He got help when he needed it. He successfully navigated the many obstacles that threatened his progress. He had integrity—a working alignment with his values and identity—which he displayed by keeping his promise, insisting on working from hope rather than fear, and by believing in his inner resources, even when they were not evident on the surface. Another hallmark of Life on Purpose is that Mortenson drew from every part of his past experience to accomplish the objective. And, the objective kept expanding, beyond anything he ever imagined in the days of the infancy of his dream. We will never be able to fully measure the scope of Mortenson's contribution to our world, but there is no question that the world is a better place with Greg Mortenson living his Life on Purpose in it.

Mortenson's story is inspiring and perhaps intimidating. We wonder why some people are able to accomplish great things. Our initial tendency is to assume that achievement at this level is only available to those rare individuals specially chosen by destiny. Or that luck is with them. These tendencies and beliefs are part, maybe the largest part, of how we stand in our own way. Arguing for our limitations we achieve them instead of our greatness. Curiosity about and respect for that inherent greatness is what pulled me onto the path that eventually led me to where I am today.

Stories

Author's Story

I started with a simple dream: to become a Dominican Sister. The spiritual environment of the convent would provide the opportunity and training for me to experience the depths of my being and unfold my greatness. After a period of several years, that was not to be the case. I made the decision to move on.

After leaving the convent, I enrolled in VISTA (Volunteers In Service To America), assigned to work as a community organizer in Poor Bottom, Kentucky, near Pikeville, upon completing my training in Big Stone Gap, Virginia. The community of Poor Bottom lived in houses, some shacks, along each side of the only road as it wandered up the mountain. At the bottom of the mountain the road was navigable by car. Flowing mountain streams, which framed the road on both sides, washed away much of the road progressively as you ascended the mountain. The road was barely a foot path as you approached the top.

Repairing the road was the project we needed to work on immediately. Possibly the streams alongside the road could be redirected to protect the road from continual erosion. We identified the appropriate official we could meet with in Pikeville about repairing the road. Accompanied by a representative group from the community in Poor Bottom, we presented our case to the official. Soon after we began talking, he started shaking his head. "No," he said, "we have no funds that we can allocate to that project." The heads, shoulders, and spirits of everyone in our group slumped in defeat. For them, it was over. They quickly accepted the official's "No" and his explanation that there were no funds. Leaving his office I gathered the group around me and said, "This is not over. This is only our first attempt. We will find other people to talk to. We will get this road repaired." They could not hear me. Regardless of how the deteriorating road severely disrupted their lives, my neighbors were incapable of conceiving of the possibility of a different outcome. They turned away and walked listlessly down the hall. This was my first realization of the "poverty of spirit" that can result from the bare subsistence of living characteristic of dire poverty. My neighbors were unable to see beyond the obvious obstacle to alternative possibilities and outcomes. Soon thereafter I had to leave Appalachia to attend to a medical problem.

Attending to this problem, I had time to think about my next step—science. Science afforded me techniques and equipment, microscopes of all kinds, to peer deeply and explore the intricate mechanisms of physical life. The body held its own mysteries about our life force expressed in the workings of our cells. Comprehending how the body's story played into the potential of our larger human story, my passion and desire to know more drew me into science.

The desire to help others realize their potential urged me to take a position as Chair and Director of Research in higher education. Accepting the appointment as Chair of Anatomy and Cellular Biology for Tufts University Schools of Medicine, Dental Medicine and Veterinary Medicine and the role of Center Director of a National Institute of Health, Research Facility, serving faculty on three of Tufts campuses, Boston, Medford, and Grafton, I wanted to help faculty develop their careers. The first two years provided opportunities to create a multimedia center to bring the use of interactive computers into courses about neuroscience, gross anatomy, and histology and engage in an entrepreneurial program with Astra Pharmaceuticals to test these ideas in classes developed for their representatives. At the same time other grants allowed us to bring new equipment facilities, including confocal microscopy, electron microscopy, and a shared core facility to provide services allowing faculty to expand their research in new directions and learn new skills and procedures. When this was all done however, the day to day demands of three deans and shrinking budgets which required continuous modifications prevented me from spending any significant time in faculty development. As years three, four, and five of my chairmanship rolled around, I increasingly became aware of the restrictive environment in which I operated and increasingly chafed at the limitations.

Upon first taking the position, I vowed to re-evaluate after a five year period. Growing discontent emerged from a feeling that I could not bring all of who I was into functioning as Chair. I took a sabbatical and then a year's leave of absence to explore my life.

Academia had been the one constant in my life from the time I was seventeen until leaving Tufts for early retirement. It had sustained me for decades, yet began to strangle me in the later years. When I drove away from Tufts Medical School, August 29, 1997, I would not return. The dream had run dry, sterile, and overstayed. I yearned to feel the joy of vitality in the depths of my being, sense the flow of energy, thrive in a supporting environment and craft a meaningful new direction for my work. It was time to get in touch with the deeper part of myself, the neglected part of myself and vitalize a new dream.

"Who is there? What's left if I strip away my roles?" I asked these questions in my search to know who I was. I had no idea how to do this. A friend told me about a writing class on Monhegan Island, off the coast of Maine. This small, isolated, rocky island, scarcely a square mile in area, accessible only by boat with no cars or paved roads and populated by artists, beckoned me. Possibly, in the midst of the beauty of its wilderness, sunrises on one side of the island and sunsets on the other, and the unhurried pace of the island, discovery of parts of me so long neglected would come forth. Over the four days of the writing class our instructor, a deeply insightful woman, provided instructions and exercises for writing during classes held in the morning. In the afternoon, we scattered to various parts of the island to explore our inner landscape and write. We would settle in for an afternoon of writing at favorite spots among the rocks lining the seashore where the smell of the ocean and sound of the waves breaking on the rocks brought inspiration. In the evening after supper, we gathered to hear each other's writings. The first thing I wrote was a poem, "Who's There?" In the poem I asked, "Who is it that is so afraid of revealing itself?" Only later did I realize I had not used a personal pronoun, but the impersonal "it." This realization confirmed how far I had strayed from knowing the essence of who I was. "Who's There?" marked the beginning of my journey.

A few weeks later my husband had a meeting on the Big Island of Hawaii, my favorite Hawaiian island. The idea of going to another beautiful, natural place caught my attention. An opportunity to continue my exploration of myself through writing excited me. My self-knowledge must precede any other exploration in my journey to find a new dream. I discovered Kalani Oceanside Retreat Village, south of Pahoa on the Hilo side of the island, close to the active plume Waikupanaha, on the ocean, surrounded by the oldest tropical foliage on the island. Kalani, a haven for artists, attracted a writer who was offering a writing course just after my husband's meeting. My plan quickly developed, I would go with my husband to his meeting and then stay an extra week at Kalani to take the writing course. Once again instruction in writing was given in the morning and the afternoon provided time for us to write. The evening was devoted to reading our writings to the four participants and the instructor.

Writing provided a microscopic exploratory view into the mystery of who I was and what motivated me to take certain actions. What was I searching for in the convent? Working in VISTA? Applying for and attending graduate school? Or, becoming an academician at Tufts University?

The writing continued and slowly revealed the theme of my belief, until finally it sprang forth with startlingly clarity. I believed in potential, people's potential for greatness, and that belief drew me to certain types of work. While I was not all I wanted to be, at that moment in time, I could create who I wanted to be. I yearned to recreate myself from my greatness. This was the potential that called me, the theme behind my drive to dream. I wanted to realize the potential of a fulfilling dream—my dreams, your dreams, and everyone's dreams.

About this time, the profession of coaching gained increasing recognition in the United States. A dream of becoming a coach began to form. A friend introduced me to a coaching organization, the New England chapter of the International Coach Federation, and brought me to my first meeting. Allured by the possibility of helping people dream their dreams and evoke their greatness, I attended several meetings with coaches to learn what they did; interviewing heads of coaching schools to find out what coaching was, as a profession, and how their organizations trained coaches; interviewing professional coaches to find out what they liked or did not like about the day to day business of coaching, what requirements they thought prospective coaches should have to be successful, and what training they would recommend based on their experience.

My past and present dreams revealed how my dreams drew forth more and more of my essential being, parts of myself not known before entering the convent or serving in VISTA or exploring as a scientist or leading a department or a research center. Exploring each of these multiple aspects of my being contributed to my next step and ultimately to my dream of coaching.

Each time I left, the convent, academia, two husbands, I started life anew. I searched for new directions, directions that would fill my being and allow me to be all that I was. I have found that and live it today, every day, with my husband of more than thirty years. This is the significance of my life stories: knowing it's possible to live integrating all the parts of one's self, as a whole and complete human being, capable of making a contribution to the world. This flames the passion.

One day the fog lifted and I knew I would find my way, I did not know how. I did not believe that someone would show me how. I just knew I would. And I did. How? By taking each step, step by step, and trusting what I experienced as I took each step. I let life live me. I let go. I trusted the process of my life.

Have I missed the creativity of science and the medical school environment? It is readily answered. Never before have I felt as free in the expression of my full being as I do today as coach, coach trainer, speaker, and author. I feel as though everything I have ever done has prepared me for my life today. What I experience is a sense of deep, meaningful contribution. It is an absolute joy to live and work from a Life on Purpose.

If we dissect this part of my story, we discover some similarities between Mortenson's story and my own. The similarities are strong clues to what purpose is all about. We were both moved by the poverty we saw around us: Mortenson by the poverty of circumstance in the Himalayas, and I by the poverty of spirit I encountered in Appalachia. We both were motivated by a desire to help others realize more of their potential. There were certain gaps in each of our ready resources of knowledge or funding that we developed a plan and took action to correct. Both of us continued to take the next steps in the direction of our goal. We both had obstacles to navigate around. We both kept going until we achieved what we thought was the objective. Both of us found that the objective grew and expanded as time went on, with doors opening in unexpected and synchronistic ways. Both of us had to use multiple aspects of our past experience. We both found ways to integrate all the parts of our being in order to make a contribution to the world. Neither of us fell into the trap of trying to continue to use outdated patterns. We looked for new ways of thinking about the challenges confronting us. Both of us discovered that by helping others realize more of their potential, we each realized more of our own. Probably the most important similarity is that we both have a deep respect and appreciation for the tremendous potential inherent in every human, including ourselves.

We see some methodologies that we might expect in the pursuit of dreams and goals: persistence, courage, moving one step at a time in the direction of the goal, enlisting help, having a plan, taking action—and these are all worthy steps that interweave with the bigger picture.

But what is it that takes the pursuit of a goal or a dream into the sphere of living on Purpose with a capital P? What makes Life on Purpose different from living with volition and determination? What are the aspects that take "merely" achieving goals into the range of our highest calling? In story after story, people achieving great things would agree they have the following components in common:

- A deep yearning for something more, something better, something greater, something grander, something kinder than what we see around us

- The energizing power of passion

- The power of compassion for others

- The joy of making a significant contribution

- Mutual benefit for the helper and those helped

- Integration of multiple aspects of an individual

- Transcends artificial boundaries

- Alignment of identity and values with vision and actions

- A sense of being involved in something larger than the individual self

- Belief in or a knowing of the greatness inherent in the human

- The expanding nature of this path

These components will be the compass, the guidance, we will use for our journey of discovery. Whether you are planning to apply for a promotion in your job or whether you are wanting to change the world with your vision of hope or whether you are making a transition somewhere in between—you will recapture more of the joy of living, more energy, more sense of meaning, if you will first consider the principles we present in these pages.

> *I realized that my identity was not defined by the roles I have played. These are what we **do**, not who we **are**. To understand our greatness, I realized I had to examine much more than just our roles.*

The first question that stopped me in my story was, "Who is there if I strip away my roles?" I could not continue until I came to some understanding that I was much more than I had previously believed. I had thought I would encounter my greatness and your greatness within the roles of our work. But I realized that I didn't know who I was underneath all the trappings, degrees, labels, and credentials of outer life, and if I didn't know who I was, I couldn't get to who you were either.

Cellular Wisdom at Work

Cellular wisdom—knowing who you are, what to do and acting accordingly— comes from the same place as your greatness. In that place you know the magnificence of who you are. You understand from this place that you are akin, to at least a tiny degree which is saying a lot, to the expansive qualities of the essence of life ageless, timeless, omniscient, limitless, and infinitely creative. Just as all the knowledge your body needs to grow, mature, reproduce, and maintain health are coded within your DNA, so do you contain all the resources you need to create, realize, and maintain a dream as the vehicle for your Purpose.

How do we know that the human is infused with the expansive qualities of life? One has only to see the evidence of it expressed in the lives of the pioneering individuals who are already at work writing a new story. It is a fairly simple process: look inside for evidence of expansive life, build a dream based upon that evidence, take action in alignment with that evidence and the dream, get out of your own way, trust the process, and observe the results. If you find that you are experiencing greater meaning in your life, if you find that you are buoyant with joy, if you find that doors open unexpectedly in your path, if you discover more of who you are through that process every day, if you find that your dream, your capabilities, and your contribution are expanding beyond your wildest imagination—then you have evidence of the spark of life within you. This is who you are at the deepest level inside. It is the real you, the authentic you, who wants more than anything to be expressed in your life.

Not everyone is looking to save the world or start an international organization. The challenge that is before you is to apply some of the principles in this book, no matter what type of transition is before you. Once you are living your Life on Purpose—not living by default—doors will open where you didn't know they were going to be, and your life will begin to take on new meaning and inspiration.

It doesn't matter *what* you find that moves you. The "what" is yours to find. It may be as simple as seeking a promotion where you are now. It may be to write a book. It might be that you want to create a position for yourself uniquely suited to your abilities. Or perhaps you just want to upgrade your relationship with your current job and find more meaning in your day to day life. These are all fabulous dreams, because they each represent the fulfillment of a longing from deep inside for something more. Consider the variety of what's expressed in the following stories.

Stories

Ernie's Story

Ernie Smith owns and operates a custom embroidery business in New York. His company creates over-scaled designs, complicated large pieces of embroidery for bedcovers, headboards, wall murals, valances, and drapery, such as the borders of the grand drape at Seattle Opera House. Formerly a scenic costume and lighting designer, Ernie started the business as a service for theatrical designers, to provide them with sources that were unavailable to them either because they were out of town or because the quantities they buy are so small. Initially, he sold laces and trims to designers and costume shops across the country. In an interview Ernie told me, "Never being one to let things alone, I wanted to do things that were more interesting. I found a company going out of business who had some novelty sewing machines. I bought the sewing machines and was thrust into the embroidery business. When designer friends of mine learned that I had these machines, the business started to grow. Eventually, an interior designer who knew a costume designer found their way to us. Today, eighty percent of my business is with interior designers and museums."

Growing up in the country with his extended family who were primarily farmers, Ernie's parents had a small business renting boats to fishermen on Lake Erie in the middle of nowhere. He told me, "You learn to do everything that everyone in your family does because they are your teachers." Ernie's grandmother and mother taught him how to embroider when he was nine years old. His tea towels with embroidered dancing vegetables won ribbons at the county fair and were displayed in Woolworth's front windows, one of the sponsors of the fair. Ernie embroidered the tea towels he bought at Woolworth with his grandmother and mother's tutoring. Not restricted to embroidery, by the time he was twelve Ernie was repairing tractors, but he always had a fascination with embroidery. He also had natural drawing and painting skills. Though he wanted to be a dancer and choreographed musicals in college, Ernie spent twenty years as a theatrical designer and eight years as a college professor. When he wanted to start his own business, the embroidery business brought his skills and talents together. Ernie continues to repair all the machines in his business, some of which date back to 1878.

Eilene's Story

Stories

In her dissertation study of women transitioning in midlife, Cindy Keeran interviewed several women about their journey. Eilene, one of Cindy's subjects, reports ". . . this was the turning point for me. I watched . . . in fact I'm getting tearful just remembering it . . . I watched a video of a trained therapeutic musician playing for a hospice patient. And when I started watching that video, I started to weep. And the feeling was . . . that's me. And it was so strong."

Regarding her job in sales and marketing, Eilene remarks: "I got really tired of being that person . . . making sure everybody is doing what they're supposed to do . . . I wanted to be the person who was the comforter, and who inspires other people, and who helps people find their way."

When Eilene quit her job as director of marketing, she packed all her suits in the back of her station wagon and drove them to Goodwill. She reports: "I was just like, 'Bye, Bye!' [laughing hard] . . .

and all my pinchy high heel shoes." She was rid of her restrictive job, suits, and shoes—each one uncomfortable and causing her significant pain.

A women's group helped Eilene along her journey. Their philosophy was to "provide support for one another's spiritual life and spiritual growth." Once engaged as a music practitioner, Eilene was happier than she had ever been.

"I am so humbled by what I'm doing. It's not about me and how I feel. You have to leave that behind and be passionate about the call, the path, or whatever it is. And it's not about you. It's something larger than you. I think that's what makes it a calling. It's really bigger. And you can't help it. You can't resist it. And I've had the most unbelievable connections with people."

Stories

Catherine Rohr's Story

In 2004, Catherine Rohr, a Wall Street investor, and her husband toured a prison. This was to change their lives. Speaking "with a former inmate who started a very successful handyman business," they offered to help him with his business strategy. In the process, "we realized that inmates and executives have much more in common than one might think. We figured that if inmates' entrepreneurial passions and influential personalities were properly channeled, they could become successful and productive members of society . . ."

The idea for the Prison Entrepreneurship Program (PEP), *www.prison entrepreneurship.org,* arose in April of 2004, and by May of that year Catherine founded the Houston-based nonprofit organization to stimulate positive life transformation for executives and inmates, uniting them through entrepreneurial passion, education, and mentoring. Engaging the nation's top business and academic talent, PEP seeks ". . . to constructively redirect inmates' talents by equipping them with values-based entrepreneurial training, enabling them to productively re-enter society."

To launch PEP on a full-time basis, Catherine took a seventy-five percent pay cut from her investment work and husband Steve turned down a good job offer. They moved to the ghetto "to live among those we serve. We literally invested our entire personal savings in this program." Why? Catherine describes, "First, I saw tremendous opportunity and untapped potential in these inmates . . . human beings who had messed up, rather than hardened criminals . . . I saw these creative, bright, risk-taking, entrepreneurial individuals who were hungry for knowledge and a fresh start in life. The second reason that I developed this program is because after seeing the need, I was struck with an overwhelming sense that this was my calling in life."

She refers to her previous work as "nothing compared to what I experienced with our participants . . . it's the most rewarding work I've encountered. Making money in itself never satisfies. Equipping others to live up to their potential is incredibly satisfying. I always thought about this question: 'If I died today, why would my life matter?' I knew that the only real impact or purpose was the difference I made in the lives of others . . ." Catherine's life of meaning sustains and nourishes her work.

The impact of PEP on return-to-prison rates is evidenced by the reduction in recidivism rates from more than 50 percent, the national average, to 3.7 percent for its graduates. The program has assisted forty participants in starting their businesses. Eight hundred plus senior level executives and venture capital/private equity professionals serve as inmates' mentors and business plan judges. In addition, the program has established affiliations with twelve top-tier MBA programs, including Harvard and Stanford, whose 400+ students serve as weekly advisors for the inmates' business plans. The program's innovative work has attracted attention for several awards, and has received coverage on *NBC Nightly News* and in *The New York Times, The Washington Post, The Wall Street Journal,* and *Entrepreneur Magazine* as reported in the magazine, *Fast Company.*

Message to the Reader

Ernie explained a very important point: ". . . that everyone in your family . . . are your teachers." He successfully translated his individual talents and skills, the training from his family, and his personal passion for design into his own contribution to the design industry, perfectly and uniquely suited to him and to his customers.

Eilene was first moved by compassion and a desire to be the comforter. This desire enabled her to leave behind her own uncomfortable suits, shoes, and restrictive job and take up a new direction as a music practitioner. She bought a second-hand harp and practiced until she was quite proficient. When the hospital found out she played the instrument, they asked her to play for patients at the group relaxation sessions. From this emerged Eilene's dream of comforting and inspiring others. She found her sense of meaning from the realization that her new life was bigger than just her and how she felt, and it opened the way for "the most unbelievable connections with people."

Catherine found her contribution in working with prison inmates and helping them develop places for themselves in society through legitimate businesses. She found that it was never about the money; that money of itself could not provide satisfaction, but that equipping others to live up to their potential could.

Each of these individuals created a new place for themselves that took them beyond their previous boundaries and restrictions. They did not necessarily achieve great things as measured by society, but they each took initial steps in finding their own greatness and their lives began to transform as a result.

Many of my clients seek me out as a coach to help them understand their purpose in life and in work, bring their fullness to their work, clarify the values they hold today, and transform their current or new work into one that has meaning for them and makes a contribution to society. The initial phase of coaching consists of clarifying the outcomes they want from coaching, their purpose in life and work and the values they hold today. These are the cornerstones upon which to build meaningful and fulfilling work that goes beyond success.

Meaning exists not as a singular event. It is constructed as we engage in the ongoing process. As we unfold our path we come to understand our Purpose.

A unique juxtaposition of events, timing, and evolution put us in the right place at the right time to set the standards for a new story, and to begin to flesh out its pages. Will we try to salvage the old one, dressing it up in new clothes perhaps, cloaking it in new trendy catch-phrases that will be old hat in a few short years, or are we to seize the opportunity to start anew from a stronger, more expansive foundation?

What a story we could create, if many began to write it from the foundation of the human capacity for expansive life, wisdom, and living Life on Purpose. We hold the power of our future—my future, your future, our children's future—in our hands, now.

In case you hadn't noticed, this is not a how-to business book. You can get that information elsewhere. **This book is about doing what you were born to do: finding and engaging in a life on purpose through writing a new story for yourself, your work, and the world. This book is about life transitions, the discovery of how to get from *the old story to our new story*. This book is about finding and engaging your greatness through your work.** I hope you enjoy our time together and are inspired to seek out and engage your own greatness.

Intent into Action

Even the best-laid plans do nothing if they are never acted upon. The challenge we have put forward in these pages is making a transition from wherever you are right now to your new story. But how does one move from uncertainty and chaos to the end goal at the top of the building while creating a script that doesn't exist yet? This section is designed to help you do just that with some tools to support life-transitioning-events. Each chapter will offer you specific chapter-content of Intent Into Action.

How you choose to process each suggestion will be an individual choice. Some people find developing the big picture compelling, while others do best with lists and writing down thoughts and ideas. Some prefer to use a more internal approach, sitting quietly in contemplation or meditation. Still others get the most value from discussing the ideas with a close friend or relative. Use whatever methods work best for you.

Working with the ideas suggested for each chapter will benefit you from the moment you begin. Each process lends itself to revisiting and refining periodically, providing you with an expanding awareness of yourself, your capabilities, and the possibilities for your future.

The value will come from starting and continuing the process.

||||||||||||||||||||||||||||||||||||||||||||||||||||||||||||||||||

Intent into Action
Tools from Chapter 1: A New Story

||||||||||||||||||||||||||||||||||||||||||||||||||||||||||||||||||||||||||||||||

Before you can move toward and then into your Purpose, you will want to get an idea of what it is. In order to get a sense of *your unique Purpose,* it is important to discover those times when you may have touched the deepest truth within you, when you sensed a piece of your purpose, even fleetingly. We each have unique individual talents, abilities, and gifts. We are highly connected to these when we are children, before they fade in a barrage of "you can't do that," "who do you think you are," and "who said life was fair." We lose track long before adulthood of what we knew so well as children.

If you will look back at your childhood years and those times that you touched the deepest truth within you, (I have helped hundreds of people discover their life purpose and most of the connections made with their deeper selves was later in life.) you will find many keys to those aspects you inherently possess, that which is already in you, that you can utilize to earn money while doing what you love and what is in alignment with your purpose. Maybe you drew frequently as a child, you played school and were always the teacher, and you read books about dogs from the time you learned to read. This is already giving you valuable insight. Key words: Teacher, Art, Dogs.

What could you do with that information to explore or create a job that is uniquely suited to you? Have you thought about teaching art classes on painting dog portraits? This idea uses all three elements in a way that you could use to earn money, even if only part time. What if both of your parents were also readers? We add another key word: Books. If you combine it with your own tendencies, you might consider teaching classes on illustrating dog and animal books. Maybe your father built houses and your mother served as president of the PTA. More key words: Planning and Building, Public Speaking, and Organizing and Leading Groups. Consider a lecture or club-type activity for dog owners to plan dog houses and communities. If that sounds far-fetched to you, don't pass it off as irrelevant. In writing a new story, you are at liberty, if not *required,* to think outside the realm of "recognized" job titles or descriptions. The creativity you use will attract vitality and enthusiasm back into your life.

This is the process for determining your unique purpose. Have fun as you rediscover gems within you and watch how they play important roles in your unfolding story, as you begin to move Purposefully from chaos and uncertainty toward your goal.

- *First, get a sense of your unique abilities, starting with the jobs and activities of your parents and your interests and activities in childhood and times you felt deeply connected to yourself at any time in your life.*

- *Second, brainstorm and research ideas that express as many of those abilities as possible. For example, what job titles include dogs, drawing, and teaching? If you have a favorite search engine online, use it and see what's possible.*

- *Third, if you already have an idea you want to pursue, find all the ways your idea plugs into your background. This will solidify and validate the direction of your Purpose. The idea is to take your passions and the qualities you're naturally good at and plug them into a life on purpose that supports you in making a living. Remember, right now, all things are possible in creating your new story.*

2
The Power of Dreaming

As a tiny acorn is the seed of a giant oak tree, so a dream is the seed of a future.
—UNKNOWN

Dreams are the vehicles through which we tap our deepest resources, explore our identity, make our contribution, expand our awareness, and express being in our outer world. The dreams available are beyond number. Where a dream might take us is without limit. Our inner resources for creating and living dreams are expressions of our inner expansive life force and are infinite. There are no rules that dictate how many dreams one person might pursue. There is no regulation on the scope a given dream might realize or how many dreams a person may pursue. The

> *Dreams are visions of specific ways in which we might express our Purpose.*

only limitation we have is what we put on ourselves—our fears, faulty beliefs, and lack of alignment with our inner creative powers. Beyond these, we are only limited by the scope of our imagination. We can overcome our fears; we can change our beliefs to those that better serve us; we can learn alignment—and if we do, the scope of our imagination will begin to expand.

Can you imagine a world in which there are no dreams? In which no one allows their dreams to emerge? We would have no art, architecture, archeology, books, bridges, businesses, careers, dance, inventions, mathematics, poems, plays, science, sculpture, social reform, or theater. We would be devoid of vision and hope. Our world would exist empty of the deepest expression of our connection to our souls.

Just as a camera lens adjusts to bring an image into focus, your explorations into the dimensions of your dreams will focus and clarify not only the dreams' expression, but also your relationship with yourself and your life spark.

Cellular Wisdom at Work

The trillions of cells in our body, including muscle cells, bone cells, blood cells, neurons or nerve cells, arose from a single cell, an egg fertilized by a sperm.

The pattern of dreaming many dreams occurs even within a single cell. Early in development cells use specific portions of their genetic material, their DNA, to synthesize molecules that allow them to mature, migrate, and proliferate. Later, they use different portions of their DNA. No longer do they synthesize the earlier molecules, but new ones that allow them to communicate continuously with like and unlike cells.

The power inherent in our dreams, released, guides the unfolding of realities. During the process of dreaming, unfolding our dreams, and living new realities, we may, like our cells, bring forth aspects of ourselves that have never been expressed before. Welcome the birth of more components of yourself and their integration as you reach for new realities, new expressions of your authentic work.

Stories

Jennifer's Story

Soon after I met Jennifer in Manhattan at a workshop I conducted, she contacted me. With great frustration in her voice, she asked,

"What can I do with a Ph.D. in architecture and art history, except go into academia?" Over the many years it took Jennifer to complete her Ph.D. studies on a part-time basis, she was employed as an adjunct professor in an art institute in New York City. At the institute Jennifer felt overused, undervalued, and grossly underpaid. By the time she completed her studies and obtained her Ph.D., a future in academia held absolutely no attraction for her. In our first call Jennifer informed me in a very strong voice that she could not, and would not, tolerate an environment in which she was overused, undervalued, or underpaid. Instead, she was in search of an environment that would support her in her desire to grow and thrive. Relentlessly, however, the question, "What can I *do* with a Ph.D. in architecture and art history?" frustrated her. The question arose repeatedly. Each time it did, it would thwart her efforts to begin to search for new work. "Can you help me?" she cried. I explained that I did not help people find specific jobs, but that I would work with her to clarify what she really wanted now that a future in academia no longer attracted her.

Beginning our work together, I asked Jennifer to spend from five to ten minutes each day exploring what she would experience if she was living a dream that truly reflected her deepest desires, even though she knew nothing about the specifics of that work or career. I asked her not to look at what she wrote on previous days so that each day she would explore the question anew. Finally, after a two week period of this activity, I requested that Jennifer review what she had captured in her daily explorations. Specifically, I asked her to condense her responses into a couple of sentences, a statement that described the characteristics of the new work that would be most important to her.

Jennifer's statement highlighted what she defined as constituting the strong foundation for her new meaningful and significant work. The values she articulated included respect, so lacking in her former life, flexibility of schedule, travel as a regular part of work, the opportunity to use her expertise, and a substantial salary. I suggested Jennifer construct a version of her statement that not only described what she was looking for but that she felt comfortable sharing with appropriate family, friends, and associates, those she trusted. Diligently, Jennifer shared her vision over the following months.

About three months later Jennifer received a telephone call from a lawyer, a friend of a friend. He was creating a nonprofit organization representing the paintings of a Cuban artist who had recently died. The theme of the artist's paintings solely featured architectural designs. The lawyer was in search of someone to serve as the executor of the foundation.

Today Jennifer represents the paintings of this Cuban artist and enjoys enormous respect from her clients due to her unique understanding of the artist's architectural designs and of the importance of his contribution to the art world today. She travels from Manhattan to Cuba and Milan routinely. Her hours are flexible. She is paid a substantial salary because of her unique combination of expertise, skills, and abilities. Without knowing the specifics of the work she wanted, Jennifer focused on what she did know: how she wanted to feel and what constituted the defining foundation for her dream work. She communicated what she discovered to others so that she could make the requisite connections to propel her forward and open the door to her dream.

Joseph Jaworski's Story

Joe's world came crashing down on him one evening in 1975. Having been away for a weekend of hunting, he was just putting his gear away when his wife of twenty years told him she had something important to tell him. She wanted a divorce. She wanted him to leave that night.

Reflecting back on this event in his book, *Synchronicity: The Inner Path of Leadership*, he writes, "I didn't know it yet, but this was the opening moment of my taking a completely different path than I had previously taken, a new way of being . . . Instead of controlling life, I ultimately learned what it meant to allow life to flow through me . . . this sort of vulnerability goes with the path I am describing—the path that reveals itself as we walk."

You may recall the name "Jaworski," as Joe's father, Leon Jaworski was the Watergate Special Prosecutor. In the foreword to Joe's book, Peter Senge tells us that Leon felt the only person he could talk to without fear of compromising his investigation was his son Joe. Living with the questions they asked led Joe, after wrestling with his calling, to leave the prestigious international law firm that he helped build. Joe recounts, "At the moment I walked away from the firm, a strange thing happened. I clearly had no earthly idea how I would proceed . . . I had a great sense of internal direction and focus, and an incredible sense of freedom that I had never before felt in my life . . . I made up my mind to take one day at a time, one step at a time."

In the *Sunday Times,* he read an article by Dr. David Bohm, the theoretical physicist who wrote the book *Wholeness and the Implicate Order.* Convinced that he needed to speak with Bohm, he pursued and found his home telephone number. Bohm agreed to meet with Joe. At the end of the meeting Bohm commented, "You're on the verge of a creative movement. Just go with it. You cannot be fixed in how you're going about it, any more than you would be fixed if you were setting about to paint a great work of art. Be alert, be self-aware, so that when opportunity presents itself, you can actually rise to it."

Joe established the American Leadership Forum (ALF) to fill the need for skillful, ethical, and effective leaders with a deep sense of purposefulness, who understand the power of a group committed to common vision, understand that leadership depends upon a fundamental shift of being, a deep commitment to the dream, and a passion for serving versus being driven by the pursuit of status and power. Today more than 2,000 fellows of the ALF infuse their communities across the nation with "a new sense of commitment, understanding, and interconnectedness." *(www.alfnational.org)*

Yvonne LaFleur's Story

Yvonne LaFleur, owner of Yvonne LaFleur Designs and Fragrances in New Orleans, revealed to me in an interview that when she was four years old she traveled with her mother on a train from California to Louisiana. Her mother, recently divorced, was returning to her home in New Orleans. Yvonne's "old maid" aunts, with whom she and her mother lived, introduced her to retail. Yvonne reports she instantly fell in love with the world of retail. At home she was surrounded by sewing, clothes, fabric, and retail talk. She visited her aunts at the stores, Maison Blanche and D. H. Holmes on Canal Street. From the time she was eleven years old, Yvonne worked in these popular stores in New Orleans on thriving Canal Street. She sold fabric at D. H. Holmes for four years, even while going to college. In 1968, during her senior year in college, Yvonne walked into a small boutique and noticed an advertisement for an upcoming fashion show. She offered to coordinate the show, narrate it, and manage it for no charge.

In 1969 Yvonne went to work for the boutique owner for forty hours a week, teaching modeling classes at night in New Orleans, while doing a merchandising apprenticeship at Louisiana State University in Baton Rouge, eighty miles away. After the modeling classes, the boutique owner would drive Yvonne to the Greyhound bus station in mid-town New Orleans. Unfortunately, Yvonne would arrive after the last bus left for Baton Rouge. Too proud to acknowledge that the arrangement was inconvenient or that she could only afford the $2.65 round trip bus ticket, Yvonne would spend the night attempting to get some sleep in the bus station. No one knew that Yvonne was sleeping in the bus station, not the boutique owner or Yvonne's parents. Yvonne feared that if anyone knew her private secret she would not be able to continue doing what she so loved to do. She wanted nothing to interfere with her unfolding dream.

After graduating from LSU, Yvonne took a job in the same boutique, now full time, in hope of becoming a partner. One day in August of 1969 a gentleman came into the boutique and offered to buy the store from the owner, who declined his offer. The gentleman turned to Yvonne and asked, "How much would it cost you to start your own store?" With no business experience, no business plan, Yvonne quickly blurted out, "Ten thousand dollars." At that moment, he presented Yvonne with a stack of $100 bills—her loan. Yvonne leased a space for $535 a month. She put up drywall, built fitting rooms, added a burglar alarm system, and opened her shop on October 15th, 1969. Three years later, the owner of the building sold it to Yvonne, the only tenant in his building who had not gone bankrupt.

Yvonne discovered her passion very early in life and stayed true to it. When manufacturing and distributing to 400 stores diminished her happiness, she created a unique concept, vertical manufacturing of her collection (the grouping of unrelated elements of clothing, hats and accessories with a common merchandising theme), for her boutique. She picked out the fabric and oversaw the production, although she did not own the factory. Contact with her retail customers, whom she describes as very loyal, is what Yvonne still loves. She designs collections for her customers allowing them to expand their wardrobe over the years, incorporating new pieces with their initial items.

By 1975, six years after opening her own store, Yvonne was traveling the world, studying in Paris, procuring wonderful fabric, designing her merchandise, and manufacturing it as a private label. She distributed her label to 400 stores. However, Yvonne loved not only designing the clothes sold in the many stores, but she relished interacting with her customers who bought her collection. She made a decision. Today, Yvonne no longer distributes her private label, but maintains her collection for her store and sells directly to customers—sixty-five percent of whom are from out of state. Retail is what makes Yvonne happy. It is what fulfills her. Yvonne remains at her initial location, 8131 Hampson Street, in uptown New Orleans.

Message to the Reader

Where do dreams come from? How do we avail ourselves of discovering them? Do we have to wait for a stroke of inspiration? Do they come wrapped in a package? Are there rules for conceiving dreams?

There are several sources for dreams hinted at in the stories we have read so far, both in the three new ones above and the ones from Chapter 1. Let's examine this wide array of experiences to find clues about the sources of dreams. Consider the following:

1) Threads from the Past

Remember in Chapter 1 when I told about how each of my first dreams were only a piece of the bigger picture I eventually arrived at? In that case the new dream rose from the themes, those threads from past experiences I had. In Jennifer's case, her thread from the past was a degree in architecture and art history. Greg Mortenson's threads were from his parents' hospital and school in rural Africa. Joe Jaworski was a lawyer in his historical thread. Catherine Rohr translated the thread of her Wall Street business background into helping inmates become entrepreneurs.

2) Contrast or Need in the Present

Greg Mortenson found an unacceptable contrast in the poverty of the village that had taken him in and helped him recover from his ordeal following the failed attempt to climb K2. The need was for the children to have a safe and comfortable school building in which to expand their minds and for qualified teachers to help them do it. In Jennifer's case, the contrast was a bad job situation in which her own needs were not being met. She realized she needed respect, to have her work valued, and better pay. Catherine Rohr thought that the contrast of inmates wasting away in the prison system was unacceptable. The need was to create an outlet for their human dignity and the expansive spark of life that utilized their talents and skills. Joe Jaworski saw in the contrast of a presidential administration gone awry the need for ethical and effective leaders with a deep sense of purposefulness following the Watergate investigations. Yvonne saw a need for someone with abilities much like hers to open a store for the gentleman who arrived wanting to invest.

3) Interests, Talents, Hobbies, Training, and Skills

Remember how Ernie's personal combination of an interest in design, embroidery, theater, and tractor repair gave Ernie everything he needed for the business he eventually created, and how it was so uniquely suited to him? Or consider Yvonne's lifelong love of the retail business, sewing, clothes, and fabric added up once again to someone uniquely suited to the position that eventually came her way. My own interest and education in cellular biology and connecting with our greatness became the basis for the idea for a series of books.

4) Compassion for Others

Eilene was moved by compassion to comfort others by becoming a music practitioner. Catherine Rohr felt compassion for men wasting their lives away in the prison system. Greg Mortenson's compassion led to a legacy of helping spread peace by building schools in some of the most hostile environments on the planet. Compassion for those struggling blind to find their greatness motivated me to keep pursuing my dream.

5) Influence of Family in Early Years

Yvonne was surrounded by aunts who knew retail business, fashion, and clothing construction. Ernie's grandmother gave him a love of embroidery, his farm upbringing taught him how to repair tractors and eventually antique specialty sewing machines. Greg Mortenson grew up in Africa while his parents founded and ran a non-profit remote hospital and school for impoverished villagers (sound familiar?). He was given family-style training in dreaming big, education of the poor, and reaching out to the native populations in remote areas. Joe Jaworski's father was also a lawyer, a famous one in fact, who prosecuted Nixon, a leader who lost his way.

We learn a great deal from our families in our formative years, all of which contributes to the sum of our life's education and training. We learn from watching our family members perform their hobbies and jobs. We absorb much more information than one would think, about the language of the profession or skill, the challenges that come up, how to handle adversity, where to go for advice or information, what the steps of the job are, how to carry oneself, and on and on. And yet this is one of the most commonly overlooked but very important sources of inspiration for dreams.

6) On the Tail of a Retreating Dream

Mortenson found his new dream as he recuperated from the previous one: to place his sister's necklace on the peak of K2. In my own story I realized that I had pursued a succession of dreams, one segueing into the next.

7) A Path Reveals Itself to You—The Dream Finds You

Joe Jaworski found that when he let go to allow life to flow through him following his wife's sudden departure, he made up his mind to take one step at a time—and the dream of creating a forum for developing leaders found him. Greg Mortenson wasn't looking for a dream in the Himalayas, but he didn't turn away from it once it presented itself to him. He recognized it as his own and embraced it.

8) Opportunity Falls in Your Lap

For Jennifer, the personal development work she did on herself caused her to decide to accept nothing other than respect for herself, and three months later she got a call from a friend of a friend who offered her a position uniquely suited to her that provided the respect she had previously been missing. Yvonne was there when her employer turned down the gentleman's offer to buy her store, and Yvonne was ready when he turned to her and asked how much she would need to start her own store.

9) Attach Your Dream to That of Someone Else

Not everyone wants to start a new business or organization. Your dream might be to help support someone else's dream, one with which you resonate. You aren't "better" if you start your own venture; you aren't "deficient" or "under-achieving" if you want to work for someone else. As long as it is genuinely YOUR dream (not your mother's, your father's, or your peers') it's a worthy dream. You don't have to be an entrepreneur in order to utilize a wide range of your skills, experience, talents, family history, compassion, and desire to make a difference. You don't have to own your own business in order to discover the deeper parts of yourself. You can be about your Purpose in a supporting role. Just be aware that when you Live on Purpose, dreams tend to expand along with your perspective of what you are capable of doing.

Purpose is an amalgamation—an integration—of all of the above. The idea is to incorporate qualities or aspects of yourself from as many of them as possible to create the Purpose most suited to you, utilizing the most of who you are. Interestingly, those individuals with the most expanded dreams likewise have drawn aspects from the most categories of sources of dreams, creating the sense that everything they had done previously prepared them for the role their dream demands.

Cellular Wisdom at Work

 A fertilized ovum or egg contains all that is necessary to create a new human being. Nonetheless, unless implantation occurs and the fertilized egg receives nourishment from the uterus and the placenta, the egg cannot develop into a human being. Once implanted, the egg undergoes significant transformation as cells multiply and differentiate to form the embryo and ultimately the fetus.

Similarly, we must implant our dream in our hearts and nourish it with loving care, just as tenderly as the uterus develops an extensive blood supply to nourish the fertilized egg so that it can grow and develop.

The extraordinary synchrony of gene expression and protein production during development of the fetus in the womb guides the development of cells, tissues, and organs. Specific genes turn on and off in exquisite timing with each other to ensure optimal development. Many complex processes must occur before an egg can become a new human, but all the information required to carry out these processes is contained within the egg. Our dreams likewise contain all that is necessary to bring them to realization, we have only to nurture them along the way. As time goes by, we will find that dreams require adding and letting go, moving on to the next dream when it is time, similar to the timing of genes.

Author's story

Stories

As I explored new perspectives through writing while on sabbatical, I took part in visionary groups. Some I participated in for only a week, others for years, always with the same intention of expanding the horizon of my thinking and cultivating my dream. These activities opened different ways of envisioning my future and novel potential pathways to that future. Most were held in beautiful natural settings; nurturing environments like Monhegan Island on the coast of Maine and the Big Island of Hawai'i. In this milieu, the nurturing physical and psychological environments blended together to create a wondrous space to explore the dream of new work. I opened to the psychological space created within these groups: safe, supportive, and nurturing. I conceived of possibilities never imagined previously. My anticipation of what was possible grew, expanded, and extended far beyond the domains of previous thinking. In the protected arms of nature and these groups, my passion for living large flamed. Something was stirring, birthing within me, needing to expand. Still, I had no clear sense of what my work would be or how to create it.

The decision to return or to leave academia loomed large in my horizon, as my time away from academia lengthened. It continually grabbed my attention. One day a friend abruptly interrupted me as I was speaking about my gut-wrenching, impending decision. "Every time you talk about returning to academia," she said, "all life seems to drain from your face. Face it. You are not going back. You cannot go back. If you do, you'll die inside." The words seared through me. In that moment, I knew with startling clarity that this was the first step I must take to birth my path to new work. I needed to proclaim, "I am not going back," first to myself. This announcement would poke through the veil of confusion and unlock the gate of my path to a new life, a larger life, and a life that would nourish me every day.

The announcement was a firm commitment to my intention of finding something more rewarding. That commitment opened the way for coaching, writing, and speaking to come to my attention. Prior to that stage, I probably would not have been ready to hear or respond to the possibility of coaching, writing, and speaking as my new dream. As it was, when I first heard of coaching, with my heart open to suggestion, I was ready and able to embrace the possibility for my future. Writing offered me the opportunity to explore the greatness that formed the basis of my coaching. Speaking helped me see how people responded to the message of greatness within them.

The more I learned about coaching, the more excited I became about being a coach myself. I incubated my emerging dream of new work. Before long, I was coaching. I sensed how energizing it was to assist people in living from the largeness of their being, activating their full potential through the taking of actions to cultivate their dreams.

As I communicated my new direction to more and more people, my voice declared an intention to "help people evoke their greatness." Each time I explained what I was doing, a new excitement would well up within me. When I described my new work, I realized how little like "work" it was to me. This "work" felt like a privilege. It excited me. It infused meaning into my every activity.

> *Everything I had ever done in all my previous roles prepared me to be who I am and do what I do today.*

One of the most exciting prospects about selecting a dream is the opportunity to reinvent yourself. Once I was ready to lay aside my former identification with the roles I had played, I was in a position to decide who I now wanted to become. Right now, while you are contemplating where you might go and what you might do, is the perfect time to consider laying aside previous roles and habits of behavior, thinking, and communicating that have held you back from expressing your full potential. Draw clues from the ideal world you are beginning to envision, from your limitless internal resources, from where you *aspire* to go, not just where you think you *can* go. This is an opportunity to let go of everything that doesn't serve you in the new future you would like to inhabit. You are more than you have ever experienced yourself to be.

Message to the Reader

The dynamics of creation are the components of the process of actualization. Did you know that there are parts of the process that you *must* do and parts of the process that you *cannot* do? Let's look first at the parts you must do.

> *The very most foundational rule of life is that inner thoughts direct outer actualization.*

Spending more time thinking about all the parts of your life you don't like and why it is so bad, will direct your creative energy to create more of the parts you don't like. If, however, you spend most of your intellectual activity on your dream and your vision of it, your creative energy will be focused in the direction of creating your dream. It makes sense to pay close attention to your thoughts and to improve the quality of them.

With that underlying principle in mind, the first thing necessary is to find a dream that excites you, that gives you joy and fulfillment, if you want to pursue a Life on Purpose. Even if you don't yet know what the specific dream is, by letting your thoughts direct your creative energy you could start by thinking, "I want to find a dream that excites me and can give me joy," or "Making my best contribution to the world is what I want my dream to be," or "Help me find the path that will fill me full," or "Today I am getting closer to discovering a dream that will fulfill and express my Purpose." You get the idea. The more often you repeat your intentionally directive thought, the stronger will be the energy attached to it.

From that start, you must supply the intent, resolve, and commitment. Intent is what you plan to do, your thought, your idea, your intention. Resolve is the addition of emotion to your intention, taking the intention deeper into your subconscious and thus summoning more creative energy. Commitment is the realization that you have no choice but to follow through.

Intention = thoughts toward a plan

Resolve = thoughts plus emotion, gathering energy

Commitment = crossing the point of no return

When I announced my intention to leave the academic world, there was no turning back. I was committed from that moment to see my decision through, and it wasn't until this stage of my journey that possibilities began to present themselves as opportunities. Shortly after making my announcement, I became intrigued with the idea of coaching. Commitment was Greg Mortenson selling his car, his possessions, his climbing gear and emptying his savings and retirement accounts so he could build the school he promised. Once he took this plunge, it wasn't long before he met Dr. Hoerni and received the balance of funding he needed to build his first school. Commitment was Joe Jaworski leaving the international law firm he helped build. He didn't know what he would do from there, but he was certain that he would find his way, one step at a time. Commitment is burning your bridges—not in folly, which could lead to disaster—but in belief of your inner expansive life force.

(NOTE: Please don't take this to mean that we think you should rush out and quit your job tomorrow. We recommend reading the entire book before taking your first action step, and we have more to say in later chapters about planning, timing, and the next logical steps.)

Your active role is to dream and nurture the dream. This is analogous to planting a seed, then watering and cultivating it. When a farmer plants a garden, he puts seeds in the ground for what he wants to eat next winter. He makes sure it gets enough water so the seedlings don't die and he keeps the weeds from strangling them. Your dream is your seed, your intention, watered with determination and commitment. The weeds you must keep at bay are your thoughts of limitation, doubt, and fear.

Next comes the part that you cannot do actively. You have to wait for the right timing and allow each seed its period of gestation. Have you ever awaited the arrival of a new infant? Its due date is the best assessment of the obstetrician, but the baby always waits for its own best time to arrive, which is very seldom on the same day the doctor wrote in his calendar. Likewise, when you bake a cake, you don't put it in the oven and then expect it to be done a minute later, wondering what you did wrong and why it is still runny. The farmer doesn't run out to the garden the morning after he planted it to see if he has carrots and green beans yet. And he certainly doesn't walk away in disgust assuming that the system didn't work. He understands that he can't force the seeds to grow, all he can do is provide the optimal conditions and wait.

Once the farmer has planted, he has no choice but to trust the process. He keeps up the necessary maintenance and he lets nature take its course. Later in the summer, he harvests the fruit of the dream he had in the spring. Until then, he trusts that if he planted and nurtured carrot and green bean seeds, that later on he will have carrots and green beans, not asparagus and broccoli. He trusts that something is happening there underneath the tilled earth that will lead to a crop of carrots and green beans when the time is right. He trusts that the seeds contain the information needed for the seedlings to grow into carrots and green beans. He has done the parts he had to do and then he lets go and trusts the spark of life at the heart of the seed, the part that knows what it is and what it must become.

After you have done what you have to do and the time is right, the next steps will begin to fall into place. If you feel you have to force something to happen, you are most likely not allowing the natural period of development. If things begin to happen easily, if you notice synchronistic events taking place, if you find serendipity at play in your doings, then the time is ripe for the next step. This is the time when opportunity is likely to knock on your door. Or you might simply wake up knowing it is the right day to do the next thing. There is a fine line between moving forward with your dream and not stopping just because something goes wrong, and we will spend more time later on this. For now, look for synchronicities to herald that the time is right. When you are aligned with your true identity, have planted the seed of a dream, have nurtured it and kept the weeds at bay, when you have trust in the process—that is when things will fall into place easily for you.

I believe that the number one reason people fail in achieving their dreams (assuming they have done all their homework before beginning) is NOT allowing the time required for gestation.

The tendency is to look for external signs of actualization too soon and, when the cake is still runny or the seeds are still growing, to mistakenly decide that the system doesn't work and give up. Don't let this be the mistaken reason for the demise of your dream.

Cellular Wisdom at Work

In my experimental studies of how the brain signals ovulation, I was surprised by the dramatic changes I observed in the relationships between blood vessels, neuronal endings and supporting non-neuronal elements, at the very base of the brain, just above the pituitary gland. The process that ultimately results in ovulation begins with the release of a peptide from neuronal endings into the blood vessels at the base of the brain. Once secreted into the blood vessels, the brain hormone is transported to the pituitary, which then signals the ovary to ovulate.

Examining the brains of animals ready to ovulate, I observed changes in blood vessels, which elongated and invaded deeper into the brain tissue, compared to animals not yet ready to ovulate. The dramatic changes that occurred in preparation for ovulation involved the retraction of the non-neural elements permitting neural elements to secrete their products into blood vessels, unimpeded by any coverings. This kind of change in the brain is called "plasticity."

This hormonal-based brain plasticity begins to occur when an animal reaches puberty and terminates at menopause. Cyclic change fundamentally characterizes this process. This is only one example of many demonstrating the continual change that occurs in cells, including neurons, even in adults.

Though intimately aware of the changes in our bodies, each day in eliciting sleep, each month in females or each year in both males and females as our bodies transform in multiple ways, most of us expect our work, our Purpose, not to change over the course of our lives. This may have been true for our parents and grandparents, however, this stability does not characterize the world we live in today. We can be encouraged by the resilience of the body, its dynamics and its message that life is creative and ever expanding. Our work may go through phases, as mine did, revealing components of our dream. Ultimately, we integrate those components and create work that employs more and more of our being. We are evolving on many levels, in our consciousness and in our understanding of our work. As we activate more of who we are, it is likely that the work we find meaningful will also change, requiring expansion, letting go, and moving on as appropriate.

Being flexible and willing to make well-thought-out changes becomes more and more necessary for keeping up with a world that changes faster every day.

We will talk in other chapters about recognizing signs that it is time for you to make a change and how to plan your action steps for optimum success. The main point to remember right now is that change is not bad; staying too long in a job or staying fixed in your thinking leads to lethargy, boredom, and lack of forward momentum. Don't stay where you are just because it feels safer than moving to something new.

Message to the Reader

Trusting your dreams requires that you believe in what is not observable, today, at this moment. Every great advance in human history began as a thought in someone's mind. Trusting your dreams provides focus to light your path to opportunity.

When Yvonne went to work for the boutique owner after she finished college, she hoped to become a partner in the business. No evidence of this was needed for her to believe in her dream. Though not apparent to her in the observable world, Yvonne trusted her dream and maintained her focus sufficiently to realize her dream, receive a loan, and start her retail store. Joe Jaworski trusted that things would work out even when he couldn't see the direction at first. Ernie trusted that he would be able to provide theatrical designers with materials they might need, even in small quantities, long before his business dream was a reality. Catherine Rohr trusted that her dream was worthwhile enough to risk a seventy-five percent cut in pay so she could pursue it full time.

The Trap of Visions of Grandeur

Trusting in the unseen dream will certainly help further it, but beware of falling into the trap of visions of grandeur. This trap is completely different from having a dream that resonates with your core identity's values. It can ensnare you in an unproductive bog and short-lived dream, leaving you nowhere on your road to a Life on Purpose.

Many times as we think about and imagine an activity, career, profession, or business, the thoughts evoke emotions related to money, position, or grandeur. However, the actual doing of the work may not be as alluring as the thought of doing it.

Over the years, many young people in high school or college came to work in my lab, intrigued with the idea of medical research.

However, when they actually worked in the lab—washed the dishes, made the solutions, handled the animals, learned the procedures, collected and analyzed data which often took months—they were no longer intrigued. The dream of research allured them, but the reality of actually doing research did not.

For a dream to lead to a meaningful life, all phases of it must nourish us—not only the anticipation of living the dream, but the reality of doing the work and the ongoing activity involved in continually developing the dream over time. A fulfilling dream will fill us with meaning and energy as we go about doing the work of the dream.

To be enamored by money, power, or prestige is to bypass the foundation laid in Chapter 1. This common trap leads to frustration, boredom, anger, and fear. Does that mean that money and achievement are wrong? Of course they're not wrong. We don't mean to imply that. It does mean that any endeavor pursued from values that are not in alignment with your deepest core can lead nowhere but to a less than fulfilling end. Look around you to see dozens of examples in the lives of people you know. Our goal is to offer insight and tools to help turn that trend around and provide the means by which more people like you can realize more of your inherent greatness.

Vision, Breaking Boards, and Trajectory

True vision, not visions of grandeur, is imperative in your pursuit of a dream. Your brain can't tell the difference between what is real and what is imagined, and your vision gives your creative energy a picture of what to focus upon.

In the martial arts one sometimes sees an ordinary-looking person breaking a stack of boards or bricks. The single most important thing for that person to focus on while attempting the feat is a spot just on the other side of the obstacle. He could muster all his inner energy, he could adopt the correct stance, he could expel his breath in a loud shout, he could do everything else required of him, but if he fails to focus on the other side of the stack of whatever it is, he will not succeed. He will most likely break his hand to boot. But by adding that

> *The dream is the idea, the concept. Your vision is what you see in your mind's eye: what you will be doing, how you will do it, how those you contact will be impacted by what you do.*

single point focus at the exact spot where his success is complete, he can accomplish what appears to be impossible. In board breaking, the difference of focus between success and failure is only an inch or two apart. When you focus on the point of success on the other side of the boards or bricks, your inner creative energy pushes right past the apparent obstacles.

In the pursuit of a dream, vision provides the one-point focus. The boards or bricks represent all the things that aren't in place yet or that could go wrong, the obstacles to your success. If you focus your attention on the board, the obstacle, *that* is where your creative energy will also focus, and that is where you will be stopped. The boards represent the 580 letters and sixteen grant proposals that netted Greg Mortenson a total of $100. They represent the absence of a store of her own to Yvonne. They represent the lack of a dream, even, for Joe Jaworski or myself at one point, but each of us carried a vision of inner guidance which provided the necessary focus for us to succeed. Vision got Jennifer her one-of-a-kind job offer for the position of her dreams, in spite of having felt under-valued and not respected—her boards. Indeed, focus on the boards before him, retraction to his scholarship and denial of his request for an afternoon schedule, is what stopped Chris Langan both times. The lesson? **Keep your focus on the goal, the vision, NOT on the obstacles**.

John Scherer, the CEO of The Scherer Leadership Center in Seattle, Washington, employs the concept "West" to guide him in navigating his way. He teaches participants in his leadership programs to find and use their West. In an interview with John, he elaborated his concept of West. "For the wagon trains heading west, West was more than a compass direction . . . If you . . . sell everything and gather all your dearest people, get in a wagon and head west, it had to be more than a compass direction. It had to represent something greater—possibility, new hope, change, (a new life, the promised land of infinite opportunity). There were . . . no maps. They just . . . headed west. If they had to go around a mountain or veer off course, what did they come back to? West." West never changes. One can always find the direction west. And the trip is never about the wagon. The wagon is simply a vehicle to carry you West, toward your dream and vision of a better life.

Often, John comments, "What corporate clients talk about is not West, but the wagon, such as return on shareholder equity, profit. These are absolutely essential. You have to have a wagon. You have to have a wagon that rolls. You have to have horses, hay, food, all that stuff. But that is not what the trip is about. It's just a vehicle to help you go West."

How do you recognize what is West for you or your organization? John answers, "If your organization disappeared tomorrow, all the people went away, everything, programs, products, everything disappeared, what is the 'hole' that would be left in the world, in life, that yearns to be filled by somebody? That is West."

West, as seen in our current context, equates with your vision, the one-point-focus that will keep you on course and provide inspiration and direction when obstacles threaten to stop you. Consistently focusing on your West, your vision, will eventually be what gets you to the promised land, the land of your dreams.

Wherever you want to go, wherever West is for you, getting there does not have to be a daunting prospect if you keep the following principle in mind, even if West seems to be bigger than anything you could possibly accomplish.

Imagine if you will, an upward-climbing path laid out before you. As you walk along this path, you will periodically encounter a question that requires a decision from you. Each decision you make has two possible outcomes: that you are moving upward, one step closer to your destination, or that you are moving downward, one step further away from your destination. You might find that you take three successful steps up, then two down, then one up, then two down.

If you step back and look at the overall direction of your travel, you will get an idea of your trajectory. This is a term I am using to describe your general direction and likelihood of achieving success. If you take just a few more steps upward than down, you will reach your objective, West, but maybe rather slowly. If you take more steps down than up, you will never get where you are trying to go. You can take as many downward steps as you want, just keep in mind that this path will never get you any closer to where you wish to go. You can't make up for the quality of each decision with quantity. If you take about as many steps up as down, you aren't going anywhere, you have flat-lined. In an evolving world, staying level or at status quo is actually slipping backward by default.

Is it necessary to have every step you take be an upward one in order to arrive at West? Of course not, as long as you take more upward steps than downward. Your trail may meander in a pattern that resembles the stock market, but if you make more decisions that have a positive impact than negative, you will eventually be successful. The most important point to get from this is that no matter where you start from—where you are right now—you have the potential of changing your trajectory, for better or worse. This is great news because you never have to get stuck on this path. And it points out the importance of each and every decision you make along your way.

If you want to escalate the climb to your goal, take more care with the quality of the decisions you make along the way. Notice the outcome of each step taken. Is it moving upward or downward?

How do you know which way it's moving? You can tell by paying attention to how it feels. Does your hope and joy get stronger? It's an upward step. Does the certainty of your kinship with expansive life get clearer? It's an upward step. Do you feel less energy than when you started? It's a step down. Was the step taken in alignment with your values? It's another step up. Did the step seem to decrease your sense of meaning? Down. Require more of who you are? Up.

Cellular Wisdom at Work

 If you were to observe neurons migrating in the developing brain and trace their trajectory, you would notice that their path is not linear. The end of the neuron that is leading the way, a growth cone, moves first in one direction, then it may completely turn around or head in a different direction. It is as though it is testing the waters or sensing a chemical gradient to find its way, very similar to the process of trajectory we have described above.

Neurons that failed to make the appropriate connections perish. Similarly, those of us who fail to find the contribution that allows us to express our authentic self also fail to thrive or even perish.

Consider the effect of persistent job dissatisfaction on our sense of fulfillment and contribution to the world. In 2007 the satisfaction of workers in the US continued a decline evidenced over two decades. The Conference Board acquired this information from a representative sample of 5000 households. Further, they state, evidence of a significant reversal anytime soon is unanticipated.

At the same time, Americans are living longer and enjoying better health than any other previous generation, reported The National Institute of Aging in March of 2008.

Reflecting on these two sets of data suggests that if we fail to connect with our authentic work we can anticipate being dissatisfied for a long time. This prospect alone may inspire you to create or reengineer your career, business, or profession and move forward to decipher your trajectory for gaining fulfillment and meaning through your work.

We can see that when we add the element of time to the concept of trajectory, the stakes can feel more impactful, not always in a positive way. We also see at the cellular level that reaching the goal is actually necessary for survival. In the context of the writing of a new story in a rapidly changing world, that may be an accurate analogy for us as well.

Create a vision of you living your dream, in a future that is meaningful to you. The vision assists you in keeping your dreams in the center of your consciousness and keeping your infinite creative energy focused on your goal. Let's explore one fun way to help you do that.

Road Map to Success

Throughout the process of dreaming, it is imperative to envision your dream as *real*. Though unschooled in the ways of doing business, when Yvonne was asked, "What would it take for you to start your own business?" she readily answered. Her experience in the boutique and the confidence she gained in college combined with her knowledge that learning something new was possible, opened the door for her to see the possibilities of a dream. Had Yvonne not envisioned her dream as real, she would not have been able to answer that question and would have been deprived of the opportunity to start her own business even if she was schooled in business.

I'm reminded of the words of Joe Batten, a professional speaker in the Speaker's Hall of Fame and the man who coined the phrase "Be all that you can be" for the Army, "In the absence of a vision, there can be no clear and consistent focus. In the absence of a dream, there can be no renewal of hope. In the absence of a philosophy, there is no real meaning to work and to life itself." Keeping your dream real is the same thing as using your vision as the point of focus for moving through obstacles. Vision is how you keep the dream real.

Living your vision is the desired outcome of your trajectory.

Before leaving Boston, a coach friend and I spent a few days during the holidays at our weekend and holiday home in New Hampshire creating collages of our new lives. My collage contained mountains, bodies of water, and hordes of flowers. Today I live in the foothills of the Rocky Mountains, close to Horsetooth Reservoir on a property that was built and developed by a gardener who planted 35,000 plants. I have reproduced that collage, laminated it, and use it as a desk blotter today. It continues to inspire me.

Remember how as a teenager you nurtured and incubated your dreams? If you longed for a sports car, you searched magazines for photos of your favorite model. You watched cars on the road to spot your sports car. You studied every detail of your favorite models and could distinguish the slightest variation that differentiated your sports car from the others. You talked about what color your model would be. You put pictures up on the wall. You constantly referred to the cars no matter who you were talking to. Maybe sports cars did not interest you. Maybe you dreamed of being an NBA basketball player. You hung huge posters of Michael Jordan all over the walls of your bedroom. You watched every game he played, when you could. You watched interviews, read articles, looked for his picture everywhere. You wanted to be Michael Jordan. Fashion may have intrigued you. You imagined being a fashion designer. You scoured magazines for stories about specific designers. You knew all their names. You had a few favorites. You pursued their style, designs, and stories endlessly. Of course, you are no longer a teenager. However, the processes you engaged in have much to teach you about how to incubate your dream, today.

Envisioning your dream as real must take root in the center of your being and be present every day for you to be prepared to take advantage of opportunities that will appear, more than likely, unannounced and without fanfare.

What I did in New Hampshire and what many of us have done as teenagers I call a road map to success. This is a technique used with clients as a fun way to cement your vision into your waking consciousness by providing a visual display that can be hung in your office, on your refrigerator door, on the mirror in your bathroom, or in miniature in your wallet. The purpose of the display is to help keep your dream at the forefront of your consciousness, bypassing all the distractions and the lack of evidence of its reality. The more deeply engrained your vision becomes, the more creative energy is gathered to the increasing clarity of your focus. The more creative energy you have and the clearer your focus, the closer to manifestation is your dream.

A road map to success consists of a collection of visual representations of your dream, a collage of pictures of your ideal situation or goal. Collect pictures of your goal activity:

- Photos from magazines, the Internet, post cards
- Pictures you have drawn (artistic talent is NOT required for this to be effective)
- Artwork from greeting cards

Things to include in your visual representations:

- The activity or goal in its most ideal and completed form
- Wherever possible include yourself in the pictures

- Plenty of bright color "to increase the power and impact on your consciousness"
- Symbols that have specific meaning relevant to your dream
- Affirmative statements, such as "I live my dream of . . ." or "People clamor for more of my . . ."

Attach all of the things you collect to a piece of card stock or poster board and put it where you will see it several times a day. Pause for a moment and allow yourself to feel what it will be like when it is successfully in your life. That moment of emotional involvement will take the dream deeper into the source of your creative energy.

As you envision your dreams as more real, the actions that you can take will begin to become obvious to you. You may find yourself exploring books or network groups or other learning groups, the likes of which have never attracted you previously. Your dreams are leading you to acquire that which will help you manifest them in the observable world. Pay attention to your inner direction to take advantage of this or that opportunity. Celebrate the small steps. You are unfolding a new future.

Stories

Bill Strickland's story

That Wednesday afternoon in 1963, Bill Strickland, sixteen years old, bored by life, living in a decaying Pittsburgh neighborhood, wandered through the hallways of his high school and looked through an open classroom door. What he saw there would change his life. Never before had he seen a man absorbed in shaping a mound of clay. Bill recounts from an interview with *Fast Company (August 1998)* reporter Sarah Terry: "If ever in life there is a clairvoyant experience, I had one that day." Bill continues, "I saw a radiant and hopeful image of how the world ought to be." Intrigued by the potter's wheel, Bill has gone on to change the world. "You start with the perception that **the world is an unlimited opportunity**," Strickland says. "Then the question becomes, 'How are we going to rebuild the planet?'"

Standing before Harvard business graduate students in 1996, thirty-plus years later, Professor Jim Heskett introduced Bill as CEO and founder of the Manchester Bidwell Center in Pittsburgh, and his work with inner city kids and adults as a Harvard business school case study. Bill, however, did not consider himself a businessman at all, simply a person whose mission is "to turn people's lives around," which he has done with two different programs. After-school classes in the arts, aimed at lighting a creative fire in the heart of at-risk kids, inspiring them to stay in school, are offered by a staff of established artists and skilled instructors in The Manchester Craftsmen's Guild. The Bidwell Training Center provides state-of-the-art job training programs to give "poor and disadvantaged adults the skills and directions they need to land meaningful, good-paying jobs that provide the foundation for a much brighter future." Bill describes his journey in his book, *Make the Impossible Possible: One Man's Crusade to Inspire Others to Dream Bigger and Achieve the Extraordinary* (Crown Business, 2009).

Manchester Bidwell's success won Bill respect and support from the national business community. Bill shares the Manchester Bidwell story at conferences and seminars everywhere with leaders in the fields of business, education, government, and the arts. Jim Heskett of Harvard became interested in this success of Manchester Bidwell and thought his students could learn something from the way that Bill operates. Now Bill was standing before the students to answer their questions and offer his wisdom from the long years he spent in the trenches. Bill describes himself as "no textbook CEO." He has no MBA and never took a business course in his life. In fact he reports, "The truth is, I never set out to be a corporate executive or to run any kind of operation at all. When I started out, all I wanted was to give some kids a chance to work with clay." He was nineteen years old when he founded the Manchester Craftsmen's Guild, a tiny neighborhood arts center that eventually grew into Manchester Bidwell.

What kept Bill Strickland going through those thirty-plus years was his passion to change the world by helping people normally disempowered to take their place among the contributors to our planet. His vision of a radiant and hopeful world as it ought to be, coupled with his belief that the world holds unlimited opportunity, gave him the fire necessary to take on the question of helping to rebuild the planet.

Message to the Reader

If you look closely, you will notice that Bill Strickland understood the basics of Purpose, the infinite nature of possibility, opportunity, and inner resources. From that foundation he dared to inquire what he might do to help turn the world around. We see the expansive progression from a recognized opportunity, to a dream of doing some good, to a vision of radiance and hope, to a personal mission and a Life on Purpose.

For Bill Strickland, West was making the world a better place by helping people with limited thinking and resources expand their possibilities. West for me is evoking the greatness in all of us. Ernie's West was finding fulfillment providing large scale custom embroidery products to those who needed them. Eilene's West was providing comfort and inspiration to those with failing physical health. Catherine Rohr's West was offering hope and means to cast-outs of society. Originally, Greg Mortenson's West was keeping his word and showing gratitude to the strangers who nursed him back to health. Later it changed to promoting peace, one school at a time. Jennifer's West was receiving the job, money, and recognition she realized she deserved. Joe Jaworski's West was providing effective, ethical leadership.

Criteria of Progress

As you develop your dream and your vision of it, there are important criteria for confirming whether you are on track, or not, to a fulfilling future and a Life on Purpose. We will repeatedly refer back to the foundation in Chapter 1. Continually checking the compass of the foundation will let you know if you are getting off course so you can take steps to correct your trajectory. Imagine the compass as you ask, to what extent:

- Are you falling into old patterns of thinking and behavior?
- Are you enthused about what you are doing?
- Do you have ample reserves of energy to do what you need to do?
- Is your awareness of who you are growing?

- Are you using most of your inner resources?
- Are you making wise and thoughtful decisions and keeping your trajectory upward?
- Have you found yourself stuck in previous roles?
- Do you place unnecessary limitations on yourself?
- Is the development of your dream and vision progressing positively?

If your overall trajectory is generally upward, good for you. If your answers to the questions above are mostly positive, good for you. If you find you are struggling at any point, review the qualities of Purpose presented in Chapter 1 and take an honest look at where you can improve.

You may be reeling from the many possibilities available to you as you create or re-engineer your career, profession, or business and target a dream. The complexity and technology of our world allow us access to places across the globe, to positions that never existed before, newly emerged in many domains, and possibilities to create our own careers, businesses, or professions. Let go of the struggle to find the right path. Be present in the moment, alert but not anxious, perceptive but at peace, knowing that there is a place where you can make your unique contribution.

I encourage you to listen to the passion that is calling you to a larger life, particularly if your dream has not yet emerged as recognizable. Put yourself in safe and nurturing environments that allow you to expand the dimensions of your thinking beyond familiar patterns.

What's the right dream for you to nurture now? A vital dream—one based on the foundational principles of Purpose—infuses your actions, thoughts, and plans with exuberant energy. Your creative juices flow. Your mind eagerly recalls your dream, often every day, sometimes every hour. You envision new dimensions of its unfolding with great anticipation. You feel energized and expansive. You see, hear, or feel yourself acting out multiple scenarios, different parts of your dream. A deep sense of meaning permeates your everyday activities as you birth or unfold your dream. The feeling expressed in the words, "Yes, this is the right direction for me," often surfaces spontaneously. Each time it lifts up your spirit. You sense the dynamic flow of life.

As you nourish your dream, your dream nourishes you.

And it does so at all stages, in its beginning, unfolding, and continuing development. Your friends and family may remark, "What's going on with you? You look simply radiant." What is going on is a Life being lived on Purpose.

Intent into Action
Tools from Chapter 2: The Power of Dreaming

|||||||||||||||||||||||||||||||||||||||||||||||||||||||||||||||||||||||||||||||||||||||||||||||||||||||

Once you have an idea of the direction of your own Purpose, the next step is to distill that idea into a dream that can give you the means of expressing your purpose. Your individual dream or dreams will develop from the unique Purpose you began to glimpse in the Tools from Chapter 1.

Let's continue with our example. Your key words are: Teacher, Art, Dogs, Books, Planning and Building, Public Speaking, and Organizing and Leading Groups. With a little more contemplation you have added: Competitive Sports and Board Games. You developed a list of possible job titles or businesses focused on these activities. These descriptions include: teaching art classes on dog portraits, teaching illustration of dog and animal books, lectures on making plans for dog houses, club activities for building dog communities, workshops on building obstacle courses for competitive and back-yard dogs, paw/finger painting for dogs and their owners, and designing a board game helping dog owners expand their relationships with their pets.

You now have concrete ideas to work with. Defining your dream from all of this information will entail integrating all the ideas into a single "Mission," not unlike the mission statement of a corporation. Some examples might be: "expanding relationships with our canine friends," or "developing communities for dog lovers," or "creating new opportunities for expressing the love of dogs." These examples take all of the key words and subsequent job ideas and distills them all in a way that leaves plenty of room for expansion of the idea. Your statement or mission should resonate deeply within you, because it was built from pieces of you. Choose one that excites you. This is the essence of your dream, and it provides the foundation from which you can begin to express your unique Purpose into the outer world and from it earn your living or a portion of it. Let's say you choose "creating new opportunities for expressing the love of dogs," and it fills you with energy and enthusiasm, making you smile and come alive every time you think of it. "Of course," you think, "this is what I was meant to do." That's how you know you are on the right track.

The next step is to create a vision of yourself living your dream, which begins to make the dream more real. Perhaps you see yourself developing an organization that eventually includes all of the specific activities you discovered for job descriptions related to your Purpose: classes, lectures, workshops, clubs, and games—all dedicated to bringing dog lovers together in fun and exciting activities that you design, lead, and teach. Remember that your vision, your "West," is your compass for navigating around and through inevitable obstacles that will arise. This journey should be deeply satisfying to you, inspiring both passion and peace of mind, because your soul is gaining the expression it has long desired. Now you are working in partnership with your true essence, from your own greatness, which is what your Purpose is all about.

This is the process for developing a dream and creating a vision of you living your dream. Dreams are the vehicle we use to move from chaos to the end goal at the top of the building. Dreams inspire and propel us into our new story. The vision gives us direction.

- *Start from the foundation of your key words and develop a "mission statement."*

- *Create a vision of yourself living your dream, adding life and color to the dream.*

- *Keep the vision alive in your awareness through the use of treasure maps or other visual representations, contemplation, meditation, and frequent energizing recall.*

- *When in doubt, dream BIG!*

3

A Strength Development Plan

*Everyone has inside of him a piece of good news. The good news
is that you don't know how great you can be! How much you can
love! What you can accomplish! And what your potential is!*

—ANNE FRANK (1929–1945)

Maria's Story

Stories

Maria is a young woman deeply dissatisfied with her dead-end job
as a cashier at a local hardware store. Her hours are not only long,
opening at 6 a.m. and some days closing at 9:30 p.m., but vary from
week to week. She never knows more than a week in advance what
next week's schedule will be, making it difficult to plan doctor visits
and other essential personal care. She feels tired all the time, in fact,
she can't remember the last time she felt fresh and energetic. Once,
she was a vivacious tennis star at the state college, but she had to

drop out of in the middle of her sophomore year due to lack of funds for tuition. She complains a lot these days. She feels there is a lot to complain about. Last week the store manager laid off two more cashiers, leaving Maria with the impossible task of covering three check-out stations. If she complains openly, she might be the next to go, so she saves her frustration for her grandfather. He is always kind enough to listen to her.

One such conversation takes place on a walking path near her grandfather's home that circles the nearby lake. They sit together on a bench in the shade watching sunlight sparkle off the water. Her grandfather, after listening, suggests that if she doesn't like the world she finds herself in, maybe she should explore how to change it. He picks up a pebble that has pretty stripes through it and polishes off the dust and mud.

"But there's so much going wrong in the world. Why should I bother? How could what I do matter in the overall scheme of things?"

He thinks for a moment. "What do you perceive the 'overall scheme of things' to be?"

Maria looks at her grandfather and back at the water before she answers uncertainly. "It's like, um, well, it's kind of like all of us doing everything at once. Something like that."

The old man tosses the pebble he's been examining into the water, sending ripples across the calm surface. "Interesting," he says, spying another pebble worthy of his scrutiny. The old man tosses the pebble into the water. "What do you see happening in the lake?"

"Huh?" Maria looks at the water.

"The lake. What do you see happening out there?"

"I don't see anything at all. Except for those rocks you keep throwing in."

"Exactly!" he seems pleased with the answer she gave. "What are the rocks doing?"

"They're—going into the water?" Maria doesn't know what he wants to hear.

"And when they go in, what happens?"

She looks flustered and says almost under her breath, "Ripples?"

"Yes! Very good! You are so smart! I knew you'd get it."

"Grandpa, *what* did I get? I *don't* get it. You throw a rock in the water and it makes ripples. So what?"

He leans down and chooses another one and tosses it in. "Ripples. One tiny pebble causes a splash that creates a little circular wave that radiates into the still water next to it and makes that water send out its own circular wave that radiates to the still water beyond that. Pretty soon the whole lake is disturbed. You *do* have the means to make a difference, whether you know it or not. Remember that story you used to like me to read to you, about the princess that gets up on the wrong side of the bed and snaps at her handmaid, who grouches at the cook, who kicks the dog who bites the mail carrier . . . and by afternoon the whole kingdom is upset?"

Maria smiles at the memory. "And the king comes into her room that afternoon and tells her she can't go to the party that night because he has a riot to take care of. Long after her own mood has improved, her bad behavior from earlier comes back to haunt her."

When you create a better world for yourself, you are helping to create a better world in general.

"In fact, that's all any of us can do, because none of us can be responsible for anyone else, only ourselves. If you keep your own back yard in order and with love, the world is immediately a better place for it. If you were to make a great life for yourself, don't you think the positive ripples would affect everyone you came into contact with, everyone you made happier by doing what you do, and they in turn would spread those ripples out over the whole lake?"

"So what would I do? Where would I start?"

"I've wondered for months now why you haven't started a business out of that funky jewelry you like so much to make."

Maria's eyes light up. "Make more jewelry? And sell it? To people? Do you think anyone would buy it?" Her passion is to take a pile of polished stones, bits of ribbon, leather, and wire, and make something beautiful out of it that someone would love to wear. She has spent many, many hours at it, and then has given the results to friends for birthdays and such.

He chuckles. "The quickest way to get from point A to point B is to start where you are right now."

"I'm not sure what you mean by that, Grandpa."

"Well, it means that you have to know what all your strengths are so you can use them. And you have to know the boundaries of your strengths so you know what you will likely have to ask from others."

Maria's grandfather understands that personal responsibility is key in changing one's life and, thus, the world. Being personally responsible means that you *own* all of your strengths and accept the responsibility of growing them. You will do whatever is within your power to bring in the expertise you need. It doesn't mean you won't make errors, but you will make a supreme effort to clean up after yourself as soon as you slip up. You understand you are the only one who can write *your* story. No one else can do it for you, and by the same token, neither can you write the story of anyone else. When you have a thought, there are consequences. When you speak, your words have an effect on others. And when you act, your actions create ripples of impact. To Live on Purpose means to accept the impact you have on your world, to clean it up when an error is made, and to delight in the ways your good and positive actions create ripples of improvement in your world.

Maria's wise grandfather also understood that you cannot lose by creating a better world *for yourself.* At the least, you have improved your own conditions. At best, you will contribute to making a better world, and you will have done it by not doing one thing differently! This effect can *only* begin with you. Each person who adds his or her own improved life to the whole, makes an increasing impact, due to ripples upon ripples upon ripples. Get enough ripples going, and pretty soon you're making waves. This is the principle by which a single individual can have an effect on the workings of the entire world.

Build On Your Personal Strengths

In addition, Maria's grandfather understood that in order to get there from here, one must have a pretty solid idea of what "here" means. This is how you start from where you are to get to where you want to go. "Here" for our purposes refers to your current personal strengths.

The coach for the University of Alabama football team, known as Paul "Bear" Bryant, ONLY showed his players their successes, the plays that they executed well. During his twenty-five-year tenure as Alabama's head coach, he amassed six national championships and thirteen conference championships. He is described today as the "winningest" coach in the history of big-time college football. I find that people tend to focus more on what they call their "weaknesses" and ignore their strengths. We do this as a society. Yet, we will NEVER succeed by focusing on our weaknesses. Consider this, even if you focused completely on your weaknesses your likelihood to improve them are minimal. Whereas, if you had spent the same amount of time and energy enhancing your strengths you will soar with the eagles.[4]

Your Strengths

In our present condition . . . "We routinely use our strengths approximately seventeen percent of the time."[5]

Eighty percent plus inefficiency is a discouraging disparity. If there were a way to tap into even a small portion of the unused potential, we might find the trajectory of the species on a very different course from the current one.

Recognizing our strengths gives us access to internal resources that we normally dismiss. I am amazed at how many times people respond to a compliment about something they've done very well with the statement, "Oh, it was nothing." The amazing thing is that they don't realize that it seems like nothing to them because it is their strength. How many times have you ignored or marginalized your strengths in this same manner? When you marginalize your strengths, you minimize your personal power and devalue your impact as an individual.

The study of human strengths has re-emerged as psychologists, long intrigued with the pathology of human behavior, have turned

---

[4] Marcus Buckingham and Donald O. Clifton. *Now, Discover Your Strengths,* New York: The Free Press, 2001. Donald O. Clifton and Paula. Nelson. *Soar With Your Strengths,* New York: Delacorte Press, 1992.

[5] Marcus Buckingham. *Go, put your strengths to work. 6 powerful steps to achieve outstanding performance.,* New York: The Free Press, 2007.)

in a new direction to explore maximal functioning of healthy individuals—positive psychology—evidenced by the publication *A Psychology of Human Strengths* published by the American Psychological Association in 2003. Reviewing this collection of essays, it becomes apparent that the re-emerging concept of human strengths now encompasses a much broader holistic view of human behavior.

> *Positive affect, well being, optimism, hope, resilience, consciousness, wisdom, self-efficacy, creativity, passion for work, and meaningful purpose are viewed as components of human strengths.*

What are you discovering about the bigger you, the part of you that you brought forth because of your passion for a greater purpose, grander than a thin definition of career, profession, role, or job? Now is the appropriate time to define and assess the broader strengths defined by your life's Purpose.

Stories

Author's story

In each of the many phases of my life, a unique set of strengths developed. Intense focus on the spiritual domain as a Dominican Sister developed, particularly when actively engaged in physical work; silence kept the focus tuned within; and discipline and persistence characterized all of my activities in the community and in my work as a teacher. Training and working as a scientist prompted questions that could be answered by the scientific approach, using instruments and methodologies available to me. In my Ph.D. studies I studied FORTRAN (derived from *The IBM Mathematical Formula Translating System*), a programming language developed by IBM in the 50s for scientific and engineering applications. Not only did I use FORTRAN in my data analyses, but found that I could also use it to fulfill the requirement of a second foreign language, in addition to French. Designing valid and innovative experiments provided the opportunity to translate big problems into answerable smaller questions. Analyzing data using sophisticated computer analyses helped me hone my analytical skills over the more than thirty years of studying science. Utilizing sophisticated equipment, such as the electron microscope, confocal microscope, computerized three-dimensional reconstruction, and the dysfunction that often appeared during their use, developed skills as an expert problem solver. In acquiring data, I learned the necessity of precision. Interpreting results, I gained the ability to detect underlying relationships between disparate elements. My skills were further honed as I trained graduate students, postdoctoral fellows, and physicians to be smart, sophisticated scientists.

As much as I valued what I learned in both of these aspects of my life, an essential element was missing—my whole self. Only in this current phase of my life, did I spend the time finding out who I really was in the essential core of my authentic self. My deep yearning and longing to integrate the multiple components of myself into an expanded whole self, offered up my passion, my deep desire to help people evoke their greatness. My process of evoking my own greatness and my desire to help others initiate the same process fueled my passion. I wanted to bring forth my genius (my genuine self) to offer it in service to others. I came to understand the larger context of *Purpose* in my work and my multiple assets (strengths, power, force, and, might). My strength was my inherent capacity to manifest energy, to endure, and to resist. My power was my capacity to do work and to act. My force was the exercising of my own power. And my might was my inner power or strength in a greater and overwhelming degree to see myself through my life transitions. It took these assets to bring me to my life's work today.

Jesse's Story

Her partner in her consulting business unexpectedly revealed that he was pulling out and intended to give her his share of the business. Confused and distraught, she described herself as a failure, as having made bad business choices.

Why had she partnered with him? Yearning to escape the isolation of her solo consulting office, she sought a partner to communicate and plan with, to help her expand her market. Unfortunately the market they expanded into was one she did not know and had no great feeling for. She felt she had not done her best work with these clients. Crying, she exclaims, "I do not know what I want to do, but I am going bankrupt."

"What do you know?" I asked.

Her energy began to shift. "I know I'm smart and really good at what I do."

"Who do you want to serve," I asked.

She brightened, "I want to develop leaders and help organizations manage change effectively."

Before the call was over, Jesse identified what she calls her "authentic client target market." She outlined the functions she wants to perform in serving these clients. With restored energy she proclaimed, "This is my authentic expression, my partnership was not."

Her unsuccessful strategy of attempting to connect with a partner in a business that did not excite her or express her authentic commitment revealed her true direction. After the fact, she became aware of the internal conflict created by this partnership. However, she did not want to identify or address the conflict while the business seemed successful. Now, considering her alternative actions, she discovered that her success demanded true, authentic self-expression.

Message to the Reader

Probably the first important point to consider when assessing one's strengths, is the idea that more than eighty percent of the time we do not engage our strengths. To me that statistic points toward the reserves of human resources that go unacknowledged, unnoticed, and even unrecognized. The tendency of the human species is to focus on our shortcomings, not our incredible power, on what we consider wrong with ourselves rather than what is fabulously right. If we could get even a glimmer of the eighty percent that remains outside of our awareness, we would find that we have for the most part sold ourselves way, way short—we have been guilty of undervaluing our most precious possession: our true, authentic nature. Is it any wonder that one of the most common complaints in today's workplace is that people feel under-valued and under-appreciated? It only mirrors our own assessment of our deeper value. Getting a sense of the grandeur of the true self and all that we individually are is the goal of this section of this chapter, not for the sake of inflating the ego, but rather so you know more about what you actually have at your disposal to work with.

We share four basic layers of existence: physical, emotional, mental, and spiritual. It is important to get a new sense of the depth and scope of your power. This will likely expand your previous concept of who you are. To that end, I will present many areas to consider.

Let's begin our personal assessment with an inventory of our personal physical strengths. This category will include:

1) Talents, abilities, and proclivities

Your talents may include anything from spotting fossils in a bed of what to anyone else would appear to be plain old rocks, to finding bargains in the grocery store, to knowing exactly the right thing to say in a tense situation, to artistic expression in any one of its many forms. Don't stop with the obvious artistic expression and assume you are not talented just because you can't carry a tune or paint landscapes.

> *A talent is anything you do especially well; usually better than the majority of people around you and something you do with ease.*

It will tend to be something you don't tire of learning about, and when you are engaged in that activity you often lose track of time. It is something innate, something you were born with.

Ernie understood how to take a plain piece of fabric and create something beautiful on it with colored thread. Eilene's talent was knowing how to help people in physical discomfort feel better. Catherine Rohr recognized the good qualities in convicted criminals. Joe Jaworski was very good at bringing people together behind a common cause. Greg Mortenson could find a way around every obstacle he encountered. I happen to have a way of gleaning life lessons from the wisdom I observed in the cells of the body, in addition to talents for intense focus and precision.

2) Experience and skills, on-the-job and otherwise

This category doesn't need much explanation. Jesse had experience and skill in consulting and knew she was good at it. Catherine Rohr drew from a well of skills and experience she had gained on Wall Street. Yvonne started gaining experience and skill in fashion design and retailing at age four. Just from my years in scientific research and my Ph.D. program, I gained skills in data analysis and problem solving and experience in the scientific approach, interpreting results, and utilizing sophisticated equipment. Add to your on-the-job skills all of those you have also developed over the years in pursuing your hobbies, interests, and growing up in your particular family.

3) Physical resources: things

Anything you already have on hand that would be needed in moving forward with your vision is relevant here. Maybe you already have a home office set up, like I had, that would suffice for a consulting or coaching business. Maybe you have a basement space that could become an art studio or woodworking shop. Perhaps you already have supplies and materials for producing inventory of your innovative product. Or that computer you use for playing solitaire might be utilized in your new venture. A computer, access to the Internet, a printer, a desk, and a telephone can get you started in any number of businesses.

Last but not least in the fiscal category, you'll want to have a precise picture of your current financial status. A complete financial statement would be wonderful. Today there are financial coaches, like myself, who can help you create this statement. However, simply a report of your fiscal status and your monthly cash flow will help give you the information you will need very soon as you begin to formulate your plan of attack. This is essential information when moving into a transition period, and an honest assessment will help you make critical early decisions in moving forward that could make or break the pursuit of your dream.

Now let's take a look at emotional strengths and what that means for you. This category includes:

1) Emotional management

For some, their emotions seem to pull them around like a nose ring on a bull. Others are well aware of the power emotions play in their lives and choose to use them to their advantage. This can be a tremendous asset. We are not judging. We are simply assessing what is here now and which, if any, may be considered as strengths. If you are a person who remains calm in the midst of chaos, who can manage your emotions and stay steady in a crisis, you have a definite emotional advantage. If you are nearly always cheerful, that is an emotional strength. On the other hand, if you fly off the handle easily and frequently or have periodic dark moods, you are not managing your emotions effectively. For the sake of assessment, think about what it is that sets you off, how easily, and how often. This will give you something of a gauge of your emotional control and how much of a strength it is for you.

2) Risk propensity

Your willingness to take risks is something you should know about. If you are very cautious and unnerved by risky situations, you may consider life to be deadly serious and are fearful of making mistakes. If you are a bold risk-taker and jump frequently into situations where the outcome is uncertain without further consideration of the potential consequences or rewards, this is something for you to know as well. It will serve you extremely well if you are someone who can consider a situation, weigh the potential benefits and costs, factor in the likelihood of a successful outcome based on sound reasoning, and take the risk accordingly. If you do this regularly, you will definitely develop assets. Don't be concerned at this point about having few emotional strengths. This is learned behavior, not something you were born with, and therefore, something that you can change.

3) People and social skills

For our purposes here, I am including this in emotional strengths. It would be a great advantage if you were the sort who likes being with people, who cares about the outcome of their stories, who can make those around you feel at ease.

The next level we will examine is mental strengths. Mental strengths include:

I) Education, information, and knowledge

Pools of information and knowledge that are not currently being used in your job or career are still powerful assets. Since you are desirous of living your Life on Purpose, every speck of yourself that can potentially be tapped is a strength, even if you don't see how at this time. All of your education, relevant today or not, is once again part of your greater knowledge pool. Do you read a lot? What kinds of books do you read? Do you surf the Internet frequently? What kinds of subjects do you like to research online? What kind of knowledge did you gain as a child growing up in your particular family? Do you watch science and history programs? What about programs on cooking, home decorating, or gardening? All of these add to your overall storehouse of knowledge and are worth recognizing as assets.

I want to point out that *what you don't know* about any subject is the easiest part to correct. You can read about it, ask people you know who are experts about it, look it up online, study books and literature about the subject, or take a class. In today's information age, lack of knowledge should never stand in your way of going after something you want to do. Filling the information gap is far easier than learning a new skill, acquiring a talent, managing your emotions, or changing your risk propensity.

2) Analytical and cognitive skills

How solid is your power of reasoning and logic? Are you good at seeing the "sense" of a thing, whether it makes sense or not? This is extremely valuable in decision making activities. Do you have a knack for perusing a stack of data and drawing a conclusion from it that is sound? Are you able to define the gist of a subject quickly? Can you quantify and/or qualify bits of information and extract cohesive meaning from them? Are you a good problem solver? Can you translate bigger problems into answerable smaller questions? Every one of these traits or abilities is a huge mental strength.

3) Integrative skills and abilities

It's one thing to be able to analyze data or solve problems or extract the gist of something, and these are all great strengths to have, but it is something beyond that to be able to integrate knowledge from many different topics into a single idea. Consider the following wisdom from the human body.

Cellular Wisdom at Work

The ever-changing and dynamic state of science is evidenced everyday by the accelerating rate of scientific discoveries. Astounding marvels of the intricacies and complexities of how the human brain works are revealed as ever more sophisticated techniques are developed. Recently, differences between the workings of the human brain compared to chimpanzees were revealed. Notably, the differences were found in regions of the human brain involved in language, lacking in the chimpanzee. The structural amplifications reflect the enhanced human capacity for language, social interaction, and planning ahead.

Learning about these discoveries encouraged the capacity to integrate information from multiple and diverse sources that would come my way to help me find my path. Being capable of integrating the unobservable information rising from within, and that which was continually being discovered in the outer world, identified the deciphering of my path. I would come to know where I was going.

Today, I confidently work with clients searching for, beginning, or transitioning from one work expression in their business, career, or profession to another to discover their new direction. As the process unfolds, time and time again, I witness the human capacity to integrate hordes of information and decipher our true path.

Our ability to process information far exceeds our understanding of how we do it. Often, the very knowledge that myriad choices are available to us, immobilizes us. Let us be assured that we possess a vast array of mechanisms within our brain to process huge amounts of information under the internal guidance of our preverbal cellular wisdom.

The last layer of assets we want to consider is our qualities of character. This includes:

1) Honesty, particularly self-honesty

The ability to be honest with yourself, even if it means you might not show in the most favorable light, means you have the beginnings of personal responsibility, which we will talk about next. Personal honesty is the stepping stone to true responsibility; there is no shortcut around it.

Honesty is a choice you make, a decision about how you are going to conduct yourself through your life.

Honesty will serve you beyond value in the course of a lifetime. Honesty will help you move into the sphere of Living on Purpose. Trust is impossible without honesty and one's ability to trust oneself must begin with honesty. If you can't trust yourself, how can you expect others to trust you? If you don't trust yourself, how can you expect to trust anyone or anything?

2) Personal responsibility

It is an enormous asset. Let's highlight some of the important characteristics:

- Allows you to own your strengths and weaknesses
- Requires you to clean up after yourself when you make a mistake
- Makes the statement that you are the one who will be in charge of you

Personal responsibility is a choice you make about how you will respond to situations in your life.

- Implies that you understand your thoughts, words, and actions have impact or consequences that you may not have foreseen, but that you will deal with the fallout whenever necessary
- We can only be responsible for our own thoughts, words, and actions; we are *not* responsible for the thoughts, words, or actions of anyone else unless we are parents of small children who cannot yet take care of themselves.

3) Values

What are the most important things in your life? What do you have to gain from those things? How do you spend your time and money? Values will be the rudder you use to steer with, the guidance for making decisions. The values with the longest lasting, farthest reaching, and deepest effects are those we all really want, whether we admit it or not: love, peace, health, family, community, self-expression, self-discovery, integrity, balance, meaningful interpersonal relationships, equality, personal growth, being true to your larger self. The more of these you actually *live by*, the greater will be your personal strength. Values have been learned as a result of decisions we made about our experiences and role models, and therefore are not set in stone. They can be changed.

Values are how you prioritize your life.

Consider this from Dr. Laura Schlessinger: "You have to define success in your own way. What maintains *your* dignity and integrity and what is *your* life's plan; where do you want to put your efforts. I could be richer and more famous, but I should have to give up things that are of infinitely more value." This is an example of how to go about setting your priorities.

4) Trust

Trust in your inner resources will come easier when you get a better understanding and experience of them. It is easiest to see anything one is trying to learn in someone other than oneself, therefore we have presented many examples in the stories in these pages. Once you can see something in another, you will be a short step away from seeing it in yourself.

Trust is a decision you make to reach for something greater than what you have already encountered or seen.

5) Discipline, persistence, resolve

All of these qualities are the products of personal decisions. You can decide whether you will act with discipline, whether you will determine your life's course, whether you will keep at it until you find a way to succeed. They are all valuable assets to have. The stories we have presented thus far are filled with examples of others displaying that they made these kinds of decisions.

Your assets are everything you bring to the table that increases your overall positive value and helps you encounter your greatness, something you can use in the pursuit of life and your dreams.

At some point sit down and begin listing everything you can think of in each of these categories that is a strength. This list will enable your self-concept of your potential value as a working persona to expand considerably. It will also give you a more accurate sense of your competence, which we will talk more about later in this chapter.

It is NOT how much inner resources we have, because they are limitless and within each and every one of us, but it IS how *available* those resources are to us. The expansion of availability will increase as we develop a strength building plan. Consider these and get excited about them:

- Vision
- Courage
- Wisdom
- Creativity
- Passion
- Imagination
- Inspiration
- Innovation
- Awareness of inner self
- Opportunity, synchronicity, serendipity

These are what make our life worthwhile. Expansion of avail-ability to resources represents our access to the incredible, expansive creative energy within us all. Inner resources are what puts mean-ing back into our everyday lives. Our strength of character enables the release of our inner passion to contribute to the good of our world. Our uniqueness to a limitless 'within' provides unlimited resources of energy and good will. It is the part that can open doors and accomplish what appears to be miraculous. Self-concept of potential value is encountering our greatness so we can put it to productive work.

Mimi's Story

Living in a state of sustained exhaustion for ten years working in the corporate world, Mimi's energy increasingly drained away from her, day by day, every day. In our interview Mimi explained, "I felt boxed in. This was the only way I knew to get acceptance, approval, and validation, given my background and my education. In graduate school I was told I would only be worthy if I stayed in the domain of my education. While I was in that box I suffered from continual energy depletion. I could not look beyond the limits of the box. I had no energy to look beyond the box. Many possibilities to leave the strait-laced corporate job came to me, but I could not see them. I could not do something new or connect to people. Friends who heard about jobs called me, but I immediately discounted them. These opportunities lay outside the box I was in and my frame of reference of what was the appropriate business for me."

"I discounted the inner urgings to do something different. I would not allow those inner urgings to develop. I would not allow them to be validated. I would shut them down and vehemently push them aside. Even though my inner urgings got stronger, I made myself ignore them. I did things based on my education and my track record. I got accolades and congratulations for my work. I was told I was so successful and that I should continue on the path, living within the limits of the box. My passion was gone. Nonetheless, I continued to be successful, but only at escalating costs to me, personally. Finally, my family and people who loved me said, 'Stop! Make a choice. You are killing yourself. You are so depleted.' I experienced severe post-partum depression with my first child. I attribute that to my not allowing myself to express myself authentically, and staying in a rigidly structured career. After I left the corporate world, I had my second child. I was very happy the moment the baby was born. I had no signs of post-partum depression."

Mimi spent two years after leaving the corporate world raising her young children before her intellectual curiosity returned. Once she heard about coaching she felt the calling. Her husband remarked, "Your vibrancy is back. What is bringing it back?" The more she learned about coaching the more she realized how it would be an authentic expression of who she is. Today Mimi has an active coaching practice. She feels the passion and relishes her work every day.

Message to the Reader

Mimi's life in the corporate world, though very successful, no longer provided meaning to her. Viktor Frankl described how individuals who fail to discover a purpose in life waste away, in his exceedingly popular book (*Man's Search for Meaning.* Frankl, V. E. 1959. Boston: Beacon Press).

Mimi was well on her way to wasting away, in spite of her success. Frankl posited that to be psychologically healthy, human beings need "not a tensionless state, but rather the striving and struggling for a worthwhile goal, a freely chosen task." What Mimi chose when she entered the corporate world after graduate school no longer provided meaning ten years later, because the costs outweighed the benefits of living that life. There was no space in her psyche for the emergence of her inner resources. Her education and position, although adequate, were not enough of and by themselves. She "hungered for meaning," as was mentioned at the beginning of Chapter 1. She yearned for connection with her inner self, to be about a Life on Purpose. Her discomfort was the result of an unnourished inner self, languishing for lack of expression. Coaching provided her with a doorway to herself, and her life filled with meaning.

Stories

Francisco Bucio's Story

A resident in plastic surgery in Mexico City's General Hospital, Francisco Bucio's dream of being a surgeon was in sight. In a few years he would establish his private practice.

Then, his world fell apart, suddenly and literally. A major earthquake measuring 8.1 on the Richter Scale collapsed the fifth floor of the hospital to the ground. Trapped under tons of debris, Francisco struggled to free his right hand, crushed under a steel beam. In her book, *Unstoppable,* Cynthia Kersey describes Francisco's rise from the rubble. Four days after the earthquake, professional rescuers reached Francisco, still pinned under the steel beam. The rescuers told Francisco they would have to cut off his right hand to free him. Francisco's six brothers and father had joined the professional rescuers in the search to find Francisco. Knowing of Francisco's dream of being a surgeon, the family refused to allow the professional rescuers to cut off Francisco's crushed right hand. For three grueling hours the rescuers worked with a crane to lift the steel beam and free Francisco's hand. Rushed to the hospital, physicians hoped that the eighteen-hour surgery would restore function to Francisco's hand. As the days passed post-surgery, no function was regained. Surgeons were forced to amputate four fingers of Francisco's right hand.

Francisco would not relinquish his dream to be a surgeon. He located Dr. Harry Bunche, Chief of Microsurgery at Davies Medical Center, who pioneered the transplantation of toes to replace missing fingers. The climb out of the rubble back to his dream began with Dr. Bunche replacing Francisco's ring and little finger with two of his toes. After much hard work, Francisco could manage to button his shirt. With intensive therapy and exercise, Francisco painfully placed pegs into pegboards, and in time was able to sign his name. He was a long way from his dream, but his dream of being a surgeon was not forgotten. Months of rehabilitation resulted in Francisco's return to limited duties at the hospital. He trained as an athlete, swimming for conditioning, tying and untying thousands of knots with his "fingers," practicing suturing on his clothes, meticulously cutting his food into small pieces, and rolling rubber balls between the "fingers" of his right hand. He also trained his left hand and became ambidextrous.

Could he operate? He was soon to find out. A senior resident observed Francisco's fight to regain function, progressing from cleaning and wrapping wounds to executing simple surgical procedures such as removing moles, would provide the opportunity for Francisco to face the test. The resident asked Francisco to assist in operating on a man with a broken nose. Anticipating that his role would be to hand the resident surgical instruments, Francisco recognized his moment of truth had arrived. The resident requested that Francisco remove cartilage from the patient's rib, a very delicate procedure, to be used in reconstructing his nose. With courage, Francisco took the challenge, and in an hour had successfully performed the surgery. He recounts: "This procedure took a lot of skill and when I did it, I realized I could do anything." Today, Francisco lives his dream. The surgeon who "operates with his feet" is a respected plastic surgeon offering a full range of services in two offices in Tijuana.

Message to the Reader

As you review Francisco's process, the blueprint to allow him to rise out of the rubble becomes clear. Francisco's determination to live his dream fueled his rise out of the rubble. With surgery, therapy, rehabilitation, and practice, Francisco climbed his staircase of goals to regain the capacity to operate. Success was measured at each step by his progressive ability to utilize his "fingers" for more and more refined procedures from buttoning his shirt through cleaning and wrapping wounds, to removing moles, and finally to performing the delicate procedure of removing cartilage from a man's rib.

Francisco's story illustrates how a man with a gigantic physical liability—the loss of all but one of the fingers on his right hand—can still be outweighed if his strengths are great enough. He managed his emotional state enough that he did not let the mishap get him down to the point of abandoning his dream. He was disciplined, persistent, and determined. He trusted his inner resources. He was very strong in personal character: he was honest enough with himself that he knew he couldn't give up his dream of being a surgeon, he was responsible enough to take on years of physical therapy and took courage from each small gain in dexterity, his values helped tip the scales in his balance sheet enough that the door was open for the miraculous in his life. Francisco exemplifies the power of building on his strengths.

Beliefs

There are still a couple of points to address in this discussion about building your strengths as a stepping stone into Living on Purpose and realizing your dreams. The first has to do with your belief system.

Many of our beliefs are the result of something we misunderstood or misinterpreted at a young age. If your belief system is limiting or constricting, you will be unable to keep up with a changing world, much less effectively Live on Purpose.

Beliefs are consistent habits of thinking that what you have come to believe is the truth of your reality. Whether true or not they influence the direction of your life, for better or worse.

Several subjects in Aliki Irini Nicolaides' dissertation examination of the nature of ambiguity report their experiences, such as an internationally recognized painter, who ". . . through her persistence with the uncertainties and shocking surprises of her life . . . became more flexible."

Another subject, a consultant growing a consulting practice in leadership development, remarks, ". . . ambiguity is a signal that one needs to become more complex in order to adapt to the demands of one's environment . . . this is something that all living systems, including we human beings have to do. I think ambiguity is so valuable, though it may be threatening at first, and yet when we are able to adapt and have a more complex way of knowing, then we are better able to adapt to the demands of the more complex environment. Ambiguity is a signal that our co-construction of reality is inadequate, and we need to adapt by adopting a more complex relationship to things." Our "co-construction of reality" equates to our belief system.

A world view describes one's outlook on life, assumptions about how things are, about the nature of the world, what can be known, what can be done, and how. In his dissertation work, "The World View Assessment Instrument (WAI): The Development and Preliminary Validation of an Instrument to Assess World View Components," Mark Edward Koltko-Rivera points out that a world view "defines what goals can be sought in life . . . what goals should be pursued."

Two or more people or two or more communities with different world views may witness the same event, yet have different experiences of that event, different interpretations about what happened and the meaning of what did and did not happen. This results from the fact that we cannot directly comprehend reality, but that we view the world through "a lens of assumptions, a lens that constitutes a world view."

Our world view encompasses a broad array of beliefs, such as:

- Human beings are basically good
- Human beings are basically evil
- Human beings are neither basically good nor basically evil, but neutral
- Free will characterizes the human condition
- Our actions are determined by our circumstances, free will is a myth
- Millionaires are uncaring individuals who stepped on others to gain their millions
- Millionaires saw opportunities when others did not, and they took smart risks that paid off for them monetarily

Koltko-Rivera distinguishes world view statements as those that "involve the nature of reality (what can exist, what is possible to occur), fundamental guidelines for interpersonal relating, or beliefs about the limits of human capacities." These represent the essence of our beliefs.

Your worldview sets the stage for what you think is possible not only for humans in general, but for you in your life, and what is beyond human capacity, specifically, beyond your capacity.

We have considered many of these concepts in our previous work together. Here we become aware of considering them, en masse, as a basic orientation to our life and our work and the impact of such beliefs.

Although our beliefs have enormous impact, limiting or expanding the scope of our lives, they remain transparent to us because of our basic assumptions that they are true. Examining our worldview reveals these beliefs so that we can understand their impact on our work. We transform the way we see the world as we spot and change limiting beliefs to more empowering ones. We begin to experience a sense of vitality as the events and opportunities of our dreams quicken in the wake of adopting less limiting beliefs. We increasingly know we can meet the challenges that we will confront. This energizes us, just as the life force energizes our cells.

Cellular Wisdom at Work

The developed fetus is thrust out of the uterus to breathe for the first time, entering the world as an independent being with new life. Uterine contractions, induced by the mother's hormones, signal the imminent birth of the baby. The contractions move the baby through the birth canal toward its new life. The organs and systems of the nurtured fetus have developed during the course of pregnancy. It is ready for the challenge of living independently. In the first years of life, the infant continues to develop its systems as it learns to crawl, stand, and walk. In fact, development of the brain continues to puberty.

Birthing our dream into the world requires courage. Further development requires the independent existence of our dream in the world. It can only develop to a certain stage in our inner world. The symphony of circumstances which occur in the outer world contributes to the continual development of your dream.

Transitioning into a new life involves being thrust forward into a new awareness, to breathe a brand new life. As hormones initiate the passage of the fetus from the womb into the world, so our startling new awareness moves us into expansive views of ourselves and what we yearn to contribute to the world. A single moment of clarity might initiate a new awareness about the inadequacy of our current life, its inability to allow us to bring all of who we are to it, or the attraction of a larger dimension of meaning.

Psychologist Williard B. Frick formulated what he called the "Symbolic Growth Experience," which he defined as "conscious perception of the symbolic-metaphorical dimension of immediate experience leading to heightened awareness, the creation of meaning, and personal growth." As he studied the phenomenon he commented, "I was struck by the timing of the convergence of all of the complex variables, the environmental events and the internal forces, that give birth to some significant transformation of the personality." He speaks of the transcendence of "artificial compartments and boundaries of life." These compartments and boundaries are the result of our limiting beliefs of identity and our reality which must be transcended if we are to pursue our Purpose and give birth to our deepest dreams.

Message to the Reader

With an honest strength assessment in your hands, you are ready for the next step on the journey: determining what is missing in your strengths that will be needed to realize your dream. If you need more knowledge about a certain subject, make a note of it. If you feel you lack good people skills, make a note of it. If you need stronger financial resources, note it. If you feel that fear of the unknown might be standing in your way, note that. If you think your business skills are weak, note that. If you need better emotional control, write that down. As you become aware of beliefs that are limiting your journey into your larger Purpose, note them.

Take the entire list and note every single item that represents an area not represented by your strengths. Most of the items on your list will fit into one of the following categories:

- Something you will correct within yourself
- Something you will find in someone else who complements your strengths
- Something you will seek through life experiences to help what you might be missing as an asset

If you remember, the strengths of honesty, responsibility, values, trust, discipline, persistence, and determination are all the result of personal decision. If you feel you need to build strength in any or all of these, begin with a list of the items you want to engage more strongly in your daily activities and stay alert for information and ideas on how to do that as well as opportunities to build strength.

Those missing assets that you feel you can compensate for with another person who can fulfill that, make note of. This will be the general outline for the type of people you will want to engage as part of your team, which we will discuss in more depth in later chapters.

For those boundaries of strength that you think will need to expand, there are sources of experiential help available. Overcoming fear and expanding existing comfort zones are two of the most common.

Susan Jeffers suggests that each day we do something that widens our comfort zone, such as calling someone you're intimidated to call or asking for something you want that you've been too frightened to ask for until now. Her mantra is, "Take a risk a day." Each risk we take, each time we move out of our comfort zone, our life expands to experience more of the world. We grow more powerful and confident. The magnitude of the risks we take will expand. Take those risks that build your sense of self-worth, for these are the risks that expand your ability to deal with your fears.

For example, Bill Treasurer performed over 1500 high dives from death-defying heights as he traveled throughout the world as a member of the US High Diving Team, in spite of the fact that he was afraid of heights. What was Bill's secret? He practiced from lower heights, over and over again and gradually walked up the ladder to dive from higher and higher heights. He was able to work his way up the ladder because he had the courage to confront his fear. He tells us, "Stay present with all your fearful feelings and then . . . walk through them," in his book *Right Risk: 10 Powerful Principles for Taking Leaps with Your Life* (Berrett-Koehler, 2003). He speaks of "Courage Capability:" expanding your capacity for dealing with future fears. "Fortified with more courage, you are then capable of facing more fearful situations." It takes a degree of courage to confront and move through fear, which in turn boosts our confidence, making available more courage for continuing up the ladder to confront larger fears.

My clients who have defined their passion and purpose and are in pursuit of their new work find themselves engaging in old patterns and strategies as they begin to implement and develop their transformed work. They experience frustration. It feels to them that they're going backward and they begin to wonder whether all this investment of energy and resources has been for naught. When this occurs, I check with them regarding their response to the strengths they've identified and discern their passion and purpose in work. If these still resonate with truth for the client, we proceed to examine the strategies they are using to implement and create their work. Usually, they have employed patterns and strategies from their old lives, which are neither authentic nor aligned with their new clear vision.

While these old patterns may have worked previously to achieve what they wanted to create, this was often at a great cost, the cost of self-betrayal. Nonetheless, the tendency to retreat to a familiar pattern of behavior, particularly when things are becoming difficult, blunts the fear of the unknown. Imperceptibly sometimes, we find ourselves slipping into the comfort of the known, but ill-fitting pattern of behavior. When difficult economic conditions are widespread in the world, we may shy away from pursuing our dream and be sucked once again into work patterns that lack meaning and drain our energy. If we retreat, we will have let fear betray our authentic self and sabotage the unfolding of our dream. Don't rob the world of your unique contribution by refusing to leave what is outdated, familiar, and comfortable.

Remember Jesse and her unsuccessful strategy of attempting to connect with a partner in a business that did not excite her or express her authentic commitment revealing her true direction? Many times this reveals that clients have sunk into the comfortable and familiar use of should, even when should doesn't really serve us very well. We need to ferret out the restrictive strategies and transform them into authentic strategies aligned with our strengths, passion, and purpose. Once Jesse identified her authentic client target market and began to offer the services to these clients, her business quickly increased and she was able to offer her contribution to many.

I'm keenly aware of the tendency to fall back into old patterns. I was once beginning to prepare for a speech at the annual Endocrine Society meeting in Denver. The speech was to be given after dinner, after awards were presented, when dishes would be clanging, wine had been served; the evening was wearing on, in the middle of a week of meetings, in a sterile convention center room. When I concentrated on these limiting circumstances I was unable to create a powerful talk. Fortunately, I caught on to what I was doing and asked myself, "Joan, how are you currently aligning this preparation with your life purpose?" I had ignored my purpose as I focused on these limiting circumstances.

I recalled my life purpose: to love and help people evoke their greatness. How can I execute this life purpose in this circumstance? Almost immediately, the answer popped up inside. *Give them something of value.* As I focused, not on the limiting circumstances, but, rather, on the value I could bring, my presentation title emerged, "Are You the CEO of Your Life?" The entire presentation unfolded rapidly. On the night of the presentation I walked to the podium with a digital timer in my hand. The people in the audience appeared tired. The evening was long. "I've set the timer for twenty minutes and when this goes off I will stop, even if I am in mid sentence." Applause and laughter erupted. People relaxed because they knew I was not going to treat them as a captive audience. Amazingly, you could hear a pin drop in this large convention room during my presentation. Even the clanging of the dishes being collected was muted. After the tremendous applause as the presentation ended, many came up to me and told me, "That was what I needed to hear," and, "I thought you were speaking directly to me." When I released my old pattern of looking at limitations of the circumstances—where and when the speech would be given—and turned instead to implementing my purpose, an effective and authentic strategy allowed me to create a powerful presentation of value to the participants.

Author's Story

Stories

I jumped off a mountain and parasailed over Lake Annecy because of my fear about my future, stripped of everything I had known.

Why this action? Because I'm afraid of heights and cannot swim. If I could face my fear of heights flying over a lake and survive, I would survive outside of academics, and be able to handle whatever came my way as I went about creating a new life. This symbolic action, successfully completed, confirmed my ability to fly into an unknown future.

> *"It is not because things are difficult that we do not dare, it is because we do not dare that things are difficult."* (Seneca, Roman philosopher)

> *Fear stops most of us from activating a dream that thrusts us into a new world. Yet, if we find a way to face the fear, we liberate ourselves to craft a life, one that is truly fulfilling and meaningful to us as we bring our contribution to the world.*

As I felt the wind fill the sails I yelled out at the top of my lungs, "Ooooooooooo Laaaaaaaaaa Laaaaaaa!" In that moment, I felt supported. I knew deeply within I would be all right. My new work started that day. I had a new confidence in my future, even though I had no idea what it would be.

Parasailing, facing my fear, continued to give me confidence in the months to come as I made the necessary difficult decisions. It remains a source of confidence to this day. I keep a photograph of me sitting in the parasail on my bedroom secretary. I recall this event and its successful conclusion whenever I face significant difficulties involving the unknown.

Message to the Reader

Symbolic action reassures the brain that you can indeed survive taking an action that is outside your comfort zone. Of course, none of these activities should be attempted without expert coaching and supervision. Parasailing and high diving are examples of activities that help in overcoming fear and discovering more of your inner resources. There are many others, of which we will list a few:

- Ropes courses—a series of obstacles or feats requiring height, balance, teamwork
- Poles—climbing a fifty-foot telephone pole and maneuvering to stand upright on top, then jumping for a trapeze bar
- Fire walks—walking barefoot on hot coals without injury
- Public speaking boot camps
- Skydiving, solo or tandem

- Board breaking
- Equine, reptile, or other animal encounters
- Rock climbing
- Karaoke

With such resources available for providing experiential activities to help overcome some of our most debilitating fears and the inertia of comfort zones and old patterns, we don't need to continue living under the hypnosis these limitations induce.

> *Symbolic action is something done specifically to push past a given fear, comfort zone, or old pattern, or an action taken that represents pushing past a given fear, comfort zone, or old pattern.*

In this chapter we have discussed the idea of the ripple effect giving power to even our small individual efforts. We have taken stock of our strengths and have gotten a better sense of those we want to strengthen. We have gained better understanding of how our strengths relate to the accessibility of our expansive inner resources. And we have begun the very first steps of creating a plan for compensating for holes we might have in our strengths that will be needed for developing our dream.

The personal strength assessment gives us a snapshot of our true personal competence. It is probably much more encouraging than might have been imagined before beginning the chapter. A solid understanding of our true competence will lead to confidence, which is a stepping stone on the way to courage. As was pointed out in the Cellular Wisdom segment earlier, the birth of a new life requires courage. We have just reviewed a map of how to get to courage.

Competence → Confidence → Courage

Your conviction that you are capable of creating your new story comprises a vital element of pouring the groundwork for your success in creating your new story. While you will call upon others in various capacities to assist you in unfolding your dream, you remain at the center of your new story. Understanding that you have the capacity to do whatever is necessary to create, unfold, and sustain your dream remains at the heart of your endeavors.

Alexander D. Stajkovic posits "confidence psychologically enables the potential that is already present to unfold, and doubt keeps such potential in a psychological 'bondage' where it remains unrealized . . . Having high confidence makes it more likely that people will initiate action, pursue it, and sustain persistence because they feel certain that they can handle what they desire to do or needs to be done. Consequently, confident people are more likely to be successful performers."[6]

A very successful colleague, Maury Dobbie, former President and CEO of The Northern Colorado Economic Development Corporation, states "Competence creates confidence." Maury founded MediaTech Productions in 1994 with $900, never having worked in the industry before. She placed a sticker with a quote from Vince Lombardi on her computer monitor: "It's not whether you get knocked down; it's whether you get back up again." Dobbie commented as she received the Bravo 2002 entrepreneur award, "It's how you get up from what knocks you down . . . I get up with a very optimistic attitude [that] I can do it."

In discussing "Why the real self is important to intentional change," Scott N. Taylor defines the real self as having two attributes: accurate self-knowledge and correct assessment of competence as reported by others. Understanding the real self underlies the ability to achieve one's goals. It serves as a benchmark to measure progress toward the ideal self.

Taylor points out that the ideal self "lets one know what direction to take to create a better world for oneself" while the real self "allows a person to know what aspects of self . . . must be managed to get there." Finally, understanding the real self keeps self-deception at bay.

---

[6] Stajkovic, Alexander D. 2006. "Development of a Core Confidence-Higher Order Construct," *Journal of Applied Psychology* 91, no. 6:-1224.

Cellular Wisdom at Work

 In evolving from single celled organisms to complex multi-cellular organisms, functional capacity was greatly enhanced. Integrating the rigidity of bone to support us in standing upright, the flexibility of muscle to move our bones and the excitability of nerves to contract our muscles allows us to walk, dance, and run. The combination of the specific strengths of each of the cellular, tissue, and organ systems contributes to the enhanced repertoire of behaviors possible because of their integration. Individual cells, tissues, and organs meld their capacities to form a cohesive, independent, individual whole human being.

> *The real self reflects the strengths we routinely express in the world. The ideal self represents a full actualization and expression of our strengths and purpose in the world.*

Our unique combination of strengths, as diverse as the components of the body, can come together to form an integrated whole, our authentic and essential self, the foundation of the contribution we will make in the world.

Intent into Action
Tools from Chapter 3: The Strength Development Plan

Most everyone would like to HAVE the systems/models/organizations and financial rewards that successful people have. Many don't have trouble observing what successful people DO, but find that they don't generally get the expected results from emulating those actions. What very few, if any, realize is that in order to duplicate the model, one must BE the kind of person the successful one is. In order to HAVE, you certainly must DO, but most importantly you must first BE or BECOME a successful person *on the inside*.

Your journey from chaos into living your dream at the top of the building begins from where you are right now. To get from A to B, you have to know where A is. Point B is your dream. Once point A is known, you will have valuable information to use in drafting your plans. This starting point (A) includes all of your habits of thinking, beliefs, emotions, attitudes, and values which are encompassed by your self-image. It includes your *perceptions* of who you are, because your perceptions, particularly your misperceptions, are how you derail yourself, losing contact with the greatness and capacity for success that abide in you.

Understand that within you is the life spark out of which the universe arose. You possess internal resources in limitless abundance, but they serve you only when you access them. Creating a personal strengths building plan allows you to do two very important things: 1) to begin developing a deeper awareness of your internal assets, and 2) to see what you want to work on in order to avail yourself of more of your true inner greatness.

Take this opportunity to see what you can change in order to BE the person for whom your new story is being written, the person capable of stepping successfully into that story. Your most valuable assets are: thoughts, words, decisions, attitudes, emotions, and values that express "I can find a way to do this; the resources are in me now; yes, I can, whatever it is, I can; let's make it so everyone can win," and character traits of courage, compassion, determination, and focus. Avoid those which express, "This will never work; I can't do that (with a million excuses why you can't); I'm too afraid to try; I'm not comfortable with that; the problem is too big to change; nothing ever works for me, I'm not good enough," and character traits of doubt, fear, prejudice, and immobilization. Recognize, practice, and engage your strengths . You will gain access to your limitless inner resources, your equity.

This is the process for developing a strengths plan. Once you know your starting point, you can then begin to develop a plan that will include engaging and maximizing them.

- *First, get a sense of your personal assets, paying close attention to the most valuable ones.*

- *Second, get a sense of which ones you want to strengthen.*

- *Recognize opportunities and practice your most valuable strengths until they become second nature to you.*

- *Complement the boundaries of your strengths by the way you write your plan (next chapter).*

4
A Wise Plan

*Enthusiasm can only be aroused by two things: first, an ideal
which takes the imagination by storm, and second, a definite,
intelligible plan for carrying that ideal into practice.*

—Arnold J. Toynbee

The Next Steps

An interesting phenomenon happens when dreamers decide to go for one of their dreams. I see it in my coaching practice time and again. They try to go from here to there in only one or a few giant steps, and then wonder why they fail. The words of Robert J. McKain express it very well: "Set priorities for your goals . . . A major part of successful living lies in the ability to put first things first. Indeed, the reason most major goals are not achieved is that we spend our time doing second things first." . . . or third or tenth.

I have found that success can be achieved when we take the next step, then the next, then the next. Won't that take a lot of hard work? Absolutely. We don't mean to suggest that you can wave a wand and avoid the work. However, by adding the bonus ingredient of aligning with your inner resources before you set out, you may very well encounter an unexpected but well-timed boost somewhere along the way. And whether the boost comes or not, taking a single step at a time, the next step, makes the giant leap of realizing your dream possible.

A plan is the prioritizing of a series of "next steps" designed to get you from where you are to where you want to go.

That is why we spent an entire chapter devoted to determining where you are right now, your strengths development plan, following the chapter devoted to discovering where you want to go, your dreams. In this chapter we will discuss translating your strengths development plan and your dream into a series of next steps.

Strategies

Have you ever gone into the garage to begin a project only to discover that something else must happen before you can start what you went out there to do? You wanted to hang a rack on the wall to hold your brooms, rakes, shovels, and mops. But you see right away that you will have to move all the boxes of books that are stacked against the wall where you want to put your rack. And not only that, but you never finished putting insulation between the studs on that wall. And before you can hang the tool rack over the insulation, you have to put up the drywall that will offer some fire proofing on the insulated wall. And, of course, before you can put up the insulation and drywall you have to make at least three trips to the local hardware store for materials and supplies.

By now your thirty-minute project has suddenly and annoyingly grown into one that will take all day, but, wise one that you are, you keep the goal of an insulated and sheet-rocked wall, complete with a lovely hanger full of well organized hand tools, firmly in your inner vision, and you make a list of what has to be done so you don't miss any steps along the way. Your list will go something like this:

· Move boxes of books to the basement

- Hardware store: 1 bale R-13 insulation, 15¾ inches wide; 2 sheets drywall; 1 box 1¾ inch drywall screws; 1 box razor blades for utility knife
- Install insulation
- Install drywall
- Install tool hanger rack
- Hang tools on rack
- Sweep garage

Your list is now *a plan* for how to get from where you are to where you want to go. To create it, you used the "what has to happen before I can do that" strategy.

In this case, the steps involve looking at the garage to see what has to happen before you can hang your tool rack. The strategy includes asking questions about what else has to happen until there are no more steps left to achieve the objective. The predictable outcome in this case is a workable plan to get the job accomplished.

A strategy is a set of steps you can take that have a predictable outcome.

Author's story

Stories

They told me it would be hard learning the multiplication tables in third grade. That's what I told my father after dinner. He answered saying, ". . . but tonight we can play, tomorrow is *tomorrow*." He pulled out a box of kitchen matches. He lined them up in rows and columns. He had me count the number of groups and the number of matches in each group. We laughed and played all evening. I loved it when I told him the answer, which was right time after time. At the end of the night of playing, he told me, "You've learned the multiplication tables."

"Oh, no," I said. "I couldn't have learned them. It's supposed to be so hard."

My father went on to teach me that we only think something is hard because we haven't yet seen the key that unlocks it. If I took the time to look deeply into what I wanted to learn, I could always find the key. **Inherent in the problem is the answer.** With the key, it would be easy. In this case, the key to the multiplication tables was simple columns and rows of matches. And the key to learning them so easily was finding the play and joy in the moment.

The lesson my father taught me that night has influenced my life in many ways. I taught mathematics in high school and college; all the chemistries, except for physical chemistry, in a girls' college; and neurosciences to medical students at a university school of medicine. I thrilled to crack the nut, find the key underlying the confusing complexity, and reveal to my students the utter simplicity that underlies complexity.

I always know that regardless of observable complexities, a key to unraveling it exists, somewhere. Today I search for the linchpin to reveal the unobservable core element to my readers, clients, coaches-in-training, colleagues, friends, and associates. This "key" strategy enables me to see and find my path through complex and confusing situations.

Each of us has employed a diversity of strategies in our lives and our work to date. Since I founded Beyond Success LLC, I have come to realize what works for me. I begin with a step I find easy to implement and then allow more complex strategies to evolve in the process of implementing my easy steps.

Cellular Wisdom at Work

In many ways my step by step strategy mimics the evolutionary strategy of organisms, which began with a single cell that performed all functions and developed over time into complex multi-cellular organisms with diverse specialized cells that cooperatively function through integration.

The unfolding of complexity and enhanced function emerged organically in response to influences of the environment. Increased complexity and enhanced function underlies the evolution of molecules, such as DNA and proteins, to facilitate the functions required of complex organisms, such as the human body. Flexibility emerges as a consequence of

the availability of a greater array of molecules, cellular processes, and tissue and organ interactions leading to expanded
functionality.

In our process of unfolding our professions, careers,
or businesses, we will build greater complexity into their
inherent structure. However, the process is organic and can
be approached in a measured fashion, modeling the way the
body builds complexity.

What makes my step by step strategy successful for me is a map
which allows me to see an overview of the process. It assists me in
exploring new or unknown directions in a measured manner. I find
that by first creating this overview map, I reach my defined goals
more effortlessly and perceive new opportunities as they come into
view. With this foundation, I act when the timing is right, when I
am prepared and ready to move forward.

Message to the Reader

Don't overlook the strategy of finding the play and the joy in
daily activity. As my father demonstrated with the multiplication
tables, this of and by itself can make a difficult task seem more fun,
interesting, even easy, and can take the "chore" out of it. A sense of
play can also lighten the ponderous seriousness that often clouds our
best intentions and weighs them down, sometimes to the emotional
breaking point. Lighten up, laugh it off, find the humor, revert to
the simple joy of living that comes naturally to children and that
is integral to Purpose, and you just might find yourself having fun
at work, worrying and stressing and fretting less. What a concept.

Scenario planning, as employed by the Royal Dutch Shell group
and described by Joseph Jaworski in his book *Synchronicity: The Inner
Path of Leadership,* recognizes that it is difficult, if not impossible, for
businesses and governments "to effectively plan a long-term future."
Instead, it is necessary to learn to create and discover what he calls
"an unfolding future." The power of scenario planning lies in its
ability to help us "better perceive complex realities and to shape the
future, not only within, but beyond" the organization itself.

In South Africa, a scenario team formed in the early eighties
engaged government officials, business leaders, black community

groups, and exiled black leaders to think about the choices ahead. Would apartheid be dismantled? If so, could the country develop an open political and economic system and reenter the world community? These discussions led to an understanding by the South African people that "the course they were on was unsustainable and that they had a choice about their future." Eventually, apartheid legislation was removed from the statute books. The first multiracial elections held in 1994 put the African National Congress in power, a position they have now held for over a decade.

The strategy of scenario planning, while not predicting the future, allows planners and decision makers to explore "different possible futures that are plausible and challenging" *(www.shell.com/ scenarios)*. Their "latest energy scenarios look at the world in the next half century, linking the uncertainties we hold about the future to the decisions we must make today."

Scenario planning might be overly sophisticated for a small start-up business or someone simply looking to change jobs or careers, but it is a concept that could be used in a simplified manner and could prove extremely helpful. Basically what scenario planning does is follow various possible outcomes into the future with the objective of trying to determine what could happen, how likely is it to happen, and how much control one has on it happening. This kind of forward thinking can certainly enable even a small time business operator or job seeker to be alert to rising trends, similar to Maria and John's market research, which you will read about very shortly, and to stay ahead of an incoming wave rather than being crushed by it.

Cellular Wisdom at Work

Each cell in the body employs a host of proven effective strategies, whether it be the release of neurotransmitters from the terminals of one neuron exquisitely positioned in close proximity to the receiving end of a second neuron to excite it and carry the message forward, or the division of genetic material in chromosomes of a parent cell to generate two daughter cells.

Further, multicellular organisms have multiple strategies of communication to ensure that control mechanisms optimally regulate effective function, e.g., the activation of muscles to contract in a coordinated fashion coupled with inhibiting stimulation of opposing muscles so that they relax. This allows us to move and walk. Another example is the rhythmic secretion of hormones, bathing cells and activating ovulation or sleep.

If we change our perspective and look at a broader, more macro, level, we note how the brain developed. Physician and neuroscientist Paul McClean explains "the human forebrain has evolved and expanded to its great size while retaining the features of three basic evolutionary formations that reflect an ancestral relationship to reptiles, early mammals, and recent mammals. Radically different in chemistry and structure and in an evolutionary sense countless generations apart, the three neural assemblies constitute a hierarchy of three-brains-in-one—a triune brain."[7]

Rather than discard the ancient reptilian brain, which controls the body's vital functions such as heart rate, breathing, body temperature, and balance, the early mammalian emotional brain simply surrounded the reptilian brain and formed many connections with it to expand function, including the ability to record memories and experience emotion. In humans the cerebral hemispheres of the recent mammalian neocortex surrounds and encompasses the early mammalian and reptilian brains forming many connections with them. Nature does not discard what works, but integrates it into an expanded higher-level function. In other words, it doesn't unnecessarily reinvent the wheel every time it needs one.

We see that effective strategies create patterns of success. Start with what you know that works, and tweak, expand, or transform the strategy as needed to meet the demands of an evolving dream.

---

[7] *The Triune Brain in Evolution: Role in Paleocerebral Functions,* New York and London: Plenum Press, 1990.

Message to the Reader

Your successful strategies, as well as lessons learned from unsuccessful ones, are incalculably valuable as you translate concepts of professional, career, or business development into decisions that lead to action. Be sure to add any strategies of your own to your planning toolbox. To qualify, the steps must be easily identifiable.

All strategies you use should be measured against the guiding principle of the "Next Step." Each step should be as easy as stepping onto the next stair. If it seems hard, there are most likely steps missing, and you're trying to take too big a step all at once. Some steps, however, will demand that you stretch a bit to take them.

Stories

Maria's Story

In Chapter 3 we left Maria mulling over her grandfather's advice and produced a personal strengths sheet. It took her hours to accomplish, but when she finished she had a much clearer picture of her personal strengths, and that alone gave her more confidence in exploring the possibility of creating a business out of her jewelry making hobby. She was surprised that her strengths were much more than she expected, giving her a greater sense of her potential competence. And the fact that the boundaries of her strengths were down in black and white made them seem less threatening. Just identifying them better prepared her to begin to compensate for them.

As Maria reviews her strengths, she knows that everyone she has given jewelry to, friends and family, love it and wear it frequently. She knows she is good at what she does. She knows she has a good mind when she is motivated to apply herself. She knows she has access to her grandfather's wisdom any time she needs it. She knows that she has a talent for finding new ways of utilizing the materials she makes her jewelry out of, and she loves finding new ways to delight her friends and family. She knows she has excellent people skills and can communicate her ideas effectively, and she enjoys excellent health. Even though her energy levels have suffered recently in her job at the hardware store, she feels optimistic that her vitality will return with brighter prospects—in fact, the inquiry she has made so far has already improved her energy levels. She has several storage boxes full of the materials and supplies she uses to make the jewelry, a computer with Internet access, a printer, and a cell phone. At the emotional level, Maria knows she is calm in most situations, and it takes quite a jolt to cause her to get angry. Maria has strengths of being honest with herself, personal responsibility, values of family, love, and equality, and she can be disciplined, persistent, and determined when motivated.

Maria found herself lacking financial funds for a new venture, lacking experience in starting and running a business, cautious in risk taking, influenced by what her peers think of her, running the limiting thought-belief, and has a tendency to want to stay where it is comfortable and familiar though it is stifling the expression and creativity of her inner, larger self.

As Maria sits and contemplates what she sees before her, her personal strengths, she begins to see that she is much more—brings much more to the table—than she had previously thought. She realizes that clinging to what feels comfortable and worrying about what her friends would think if she tries to pursue her dream and fails is holding her back. She also realizes that she has had a preponderance of assets all along, but because she didn't have a perception of them, her limited view of herself prevented her from recognizing opportunities to use them. For the first time, she begins to see that starting her own business might be something she can really do.

Maria decides to begin selling jewelry after hours of her cashier job for a period of time so she can get her finances in better condition. This will give her a trial period to see how sales of her jewelry will go before cutting off her main source of income from the hardware store. This is a temporary plan for Maria to get a feel for how she would like making jewelry for a living, and, if she thinks it's going to work for her, it provides a smoother transition financially for her. The idea of not having to break off one to do the other is a huge relief to Maria and gives her additional confidence in taking these initial steps.

At the end of twelve months, with income from two sources, Maria has paid off her car loan, her only outstanding debt, and has saved a total of $6,000. The savings provide a cushion as Maria implements the second phase of her plan: reducing her hours at the hardware store so she can spend more time making and selling jewelry.

Maria realizes she has access to her brother John, who is a business whiz in his own right and lives near Maria's neighborhood. John is pleased with Maria's plans and progress so far, and he slips willingly into the mentoring position. John and Maria decide to meet to put together her ongoing plan. John tells her that their objective is simple, in the words of Denis Waitley, "Expect the best, plan for the worst and prepare to be surprised ." In essence this says to keep a positive attitude and habits of thinking, plan ahead for obstacles, and stay alert for the unexpected opportunity.

They already know that Maria's objective, her dream, is to make beautiful jewelry from interesting materials that people will love to wear. Her vision is to keep costs of production low enough that she can sell her work at reasonable prices to women of average income, providing them with something of beauty at an affordable price. She sees herself with a team of committed people around her who share her vision and help her implement her plans. She sees her product giving great pleasure and value to everyone who wears it with the demand growing beyond her wildest dreams. She sees herself growing and expanding to fit the demands of a popular venture, and not only for herself, but for all her employees as well.

They draw up a profile of the roles they are likely to need to fill in as close to the order of necessity as they can make it. John suggests that every business venture absolutely requires a good tax accountant, even at the smallest business levels. Maria already has her brother to serve as a mentor while she learns about being in business. They know that a graphic artist and/or computer wizard will be needed almost from the get-go. In Maria's specific business of supplying a product, people to make the individual items would be needed before long and possibly sales people as well.

Next, Maria and John discuss who their ideal customer is likely to be. Maria's vision offers clues on this one: average-income women who like and wear jewelry or who give jewelry as gifts. Ideally, they would find a core of customers who have a wide base of friends and acquaintances, who are influential among that network, and who like Maria's jewelry well enough to tell their network about it. These women might tend to be members of churches, clubs, sororities, PTA, or teachers' organizations. Maria goes through her contact list of friends, family, and acquaintances and notes the ones who best fit the influential networker of middle-income criteria.

After they get a good idea of their ideal target market, they discuss a variety of ways they might reach that specific market. John says that word of mouth is always one of the most effective and *the* most cost effective method of reaching people that there is. Maria suggests doing an open house to introduce her products, inviting leaders from all the women's organizations she can find in her local area, resembling a gallery opening for an artist. They decide to see if some of their friends would volunteer to help at the event. They also look at direct mailing of a flyer to people she knows inviting them to invite their friends as an option, posting notices and brochures in the local beauty salons, handing out flyers to mothers picking up kids at school, and running an ad on craigslist.com with a couple of photographs of sample items.

Reaching their target market segues directly into the topic of marketing. John tells Maria that marketing is simply a strategy or set of strategies designed to bring customers in your door, educate them about the products you offer, and keep them coming back for more. They spend a few minutes brainstorming ideas for what John calls a "two-sentence advertisement." The purpose of this is to put Maria's entire vision into no more than two sentences that could be delivered in the length of an elevator ride from the lobby to the eighth floor. After a few minutes they arrive at one they both like: "Maria's trend-setting fashion jewelry at prices everyone can afford." So anywhere Maria goes, she is prepared to answer the question when someone asks what she does for work.

The next part of Maria's plan is about how she will survive financially while she gets her new business started. She already had her phase one plan in place and accomplished—work full-time at the hardware store while making and selling jewelry on the side for a year; pay off her car loan, reducing her monthly expenses; and save a minimum of $5,000 while earning two incomes. Maria managed to exceed her savings goal by a thousand dollars. They decide together that the next phase would entail cutting back on her cashier hours to allow more time for jewelry sales and production without totally cutting off that supply of regular income.

Maria is excited about her prospects. With a sensible plan in place, she feels far better prepared to handle the various phases of developing her business. She feels like she has a series of steps to take, each one well within her capabilities to accomplish.

Message to the Reader

You will notice that the strengths development exercise caused Maria's perception of her strengths and her capabilities to shift, expanding beyond what they had been previously, which in turn opened a little doorway of possibility in her life that hadn't been there before. That tiny opening was enough to give her sufficient hope to begin to explore a future she had not dared to dream before. The exercise also gave her a starting place to begin planning how she could best proceed toward fulfilling her dream of her own jewelry business. Using the wisdom of her grandfather's and John's guidance, Maria took smart steps toward her dream that were within her means, minimizing the lack of financial resources and maximizing her financial position for going forward, rather than rushing into something she was not prepared to handle financially.

Like Maria felt about her cashier job, many of you probably feel stuck where you are and would love to encounter a "tiny opening of hope." Feeling stuck is actually an indication that change is needed. There are specific signs—red flags, if you will—that indicate when it is time for you to think about making a change in your life:

- Lack of energy
- Lack of interest
- Lack of passion
- Lack of meaning
- Lack of clarity
- Lack of being appreciated
- Lack of fulfillment
- Lack of expansion and growth
- Lack of vitality
- Lack of opportunity

What all of these lacks are really saying is that you are missing the connection to and alignment with your true inner self. The change that is needed might be to shift your perspective of yourself, not necessarily change jobs or positions. Review your personal balance sheet and think and feel deeply about them, all of them. With a deeper sense of who you really are, you will have a better foundation on which to base your decision about where you need to make changes now, whether in your relationship with your current job, pursuing a new position, career, or venture, or moving across country and starting fresh. You will only gain by learning more about who you truly are, and a personal balance sheet is a good place to start.

Let's take a closer look at the various components of a wise plan, no matter what your objective turns out to be.

1) Define the objective

What will you be doing? For corporations, this step often results in the creation of a mission statement, the concise definition of what the company plans to do and to accomplish. The company vision, equating to your dream, is *the driving concept that 'pulls' the enterprise . . . forward toward its target.* The mission includes what we do, for whom and why.[8] Vision and mission together guide the development of the business. Remember that Maria's dream was fairly simple: to create a business designing and making jewelry. Her vision was a more defined picture: creating beautiful jewelry at reasonable prices, people happily wearing the designs, Maria and her employees all growing with the demands of a popular product.

2) Analyze the market

Is there a need or at least room for your product or service in your area? In most cases this will entail nothing more than doing an Internet search to see whether your product or service is already well represented in your immediate area. The research might point out the need for a slightly different angle to create a niche for what you

---

[8] Derek F. Abell. The future of strategy is leadership. *Journal of Business Research* 59 (3):310–314, 2006.

offer, or it might bring to light the need to consider going into another area geographically. This also applies to those whose product is their personal skill, expertise, and strengths offered to an employer. The main point is this: if your area is already oversaturated with others doing what you want to do, you might need to tweak your dream or reconsider where you might seek to change jobs or start a new venture.

If you are seeking employment in today's shrinking job market, tweaking your dream might entail creating a niche for yourself that is uniquely suited to your skills, abilities, and talents. This strategy tends to negate the existing competition and make you particularly valuable to your prospective (or current) employer. What specific need does the chain of command have that suits your qualifications to a tee? Creating a position for yourself can be an exciting and rewarding venture, utilizing many of your unique strengths without requiring that you start your own business. Once you identify the combination of assets that makes you unique, present yourself just as if you were selling a product or service, sell prospective employers on the value your uniqueness can give them, and then look for the most favorable offer.

The second factor in market analysis is timing. The best idea there is will not blossom until the market is ready for your service or product. How can you tell whether the public in your market area is ripe for your innovation? If sales take off and demand grows, it was ready. If it doesn't, it might not be quite the right time yet. Hitting the peak of the incoming wave requires astute observation. Coming in too far ahead or too far behind the wave will both produce weak results. You can tell that you are behind the wave if everyone you know is already in possession of your product made or provided by someone else. If the wave hasn't started yet, trying little "feelers" into potential sales, listening for clues in casual conversation, and watching what's happening with trends will all help you get a feel for that perfect timing. Catching the wave at its peak can be breathtaking.

3) Who will you need to help you?

A wise mentor early in your planning stages can be worth her/his weight in gold. A mentor who knows the ropes of your particular dream is like training wheels on your first two-wheel bicycle. They can help you stay upright while you get the hang of what needs to be done. If you can choose someone who not only knows the ropes but who also appears to have some understanding of Living on Purpose, all the better, for you will not only have a mentor, but a role model.

A mentor in the company or field in which you might like to seek employment is worth cultivating as well. Someone on the "inside," particularly if it is a friend of a friend or an acquaintance, can help pave the way to an interview with the right individual, or might be able to give you a good character reference if they know you or your family. Or perhaps they would be able to tell you some of the current challenges some of the departments are having and could help you evaluate how you might be able to be a good match for a specific need. The company might not even have a job description or know that they need you yet, but if you can help them solve a current dilemma, they will give you every consideration possible. However, do not ignore those in your industry "outside" of the company in which you seek employment. They probably have connections within the company, but in addition, they know the reputation of the company shared within the industry, but maybe not outside of it. They can prove a valuable connection.

Every business venture and many wage earners need a good tax accountant. Every business needs a graphic designer who can help create at least a simple web presentation and at least a simple brochure or other advertising piece. A graphic designer might be able to help you create a striking resume if you are seeking employment. Nearly every business would also benefit from having access to a computer expert who can keep your technology up and running. As your business grows, depending on the nature of what you do, you may also need to add sales people and/or assembly people to make your product. If you grow even more you might find a need for managers and coordinators, an advisory board, legal representation, and a CFO for more complex financial planning. You may find helpers and professionals who are free-lance and hire out by the hour. You will perhaps pay more per hour for their services than you would for a full-time employee, but you won't have to pay for more hours than you actually need, until such time that your business requires and can support full time professionals.

As you begin to think about who might fill these roles, keep in mind the boundaries of your strengths. The people you choose to work with can help compensate for those areas beyond the boundaries of your strengths, if you choose them carefully. In Maria's case, she would be wise to look for those who are a little bolder in approaching risk, who can, for whatever reason, afford to work more reasonably while she gets up and running, who have plenty of business experience already under their belts, who exhibit insightful thinking habits, and who are not overly stuck in the inertia of their comfort zones. Not every individual will have all of these qualities, but if they are all adequately represented across the staff, Maria will have used her strengths analysis wisely in selecting people to help make her dream a reality.

4) Who will be your customers?

Identify your ideal customer or target market. This will encompass gender, age, affiliations, financial status, and any unique characteristics that would be likely to attract them to your product or service. Maria and John identified women of average income who like to wear jewelry, and ideally who have a wide network of friends and acquaintances with whom the customer has influence, who would be likely to tell their network about Maria's jewelry if they really liked it.

5) How will you reach your prospective customers?

Get the word out about your new venture understanding a few simple principles of what marketing is.

Since I knew academia and had great passion for women in academia, I decided I would initially contact *them to kick off my coaching business.* Maybe they would be ready to further their careers or maybe they would know someone who could use a coach to help them develop and execute the plan to further their careers. I planned to hire a graduate student to enter data from a membership book that listed professors' contact information into a database. I could identify potential clients and then draft a letter announcing the founding of my business. I could explain my services and ask them to contact me if they could use my services and refer others who might benefit from my services to me. Before long, plan in hand, I was on my way.

Marketing is not a mystery. The following is a recap of the basic principles that Maria and John used in developing their marketing strategy:

- Contact prospects with a description of what you offer
- Who is a prospect? *Anyone* who shows an interest—plus your target market
- Start with your two-sentence advertisement
- Get their attention by telling them what makes you different than everyone else doing what you do, three to five concise points
- Make a promise (what you can and will deliver) and guarantee it (with a time limit)
- Keep in contact with them regularly, offer coupons, punch cards, volume discounts, points toward free merchandise or services, or referral bonuses for telling their friends—make them feel good about purchasing from you more than once and make sure the rewards are all tied to actual purchases, not just visits or browsing
- *Always* use a plan that allows the results to be tracked—keep track of which methods of advertising are actually bringing in buying customers or clients before investing too much money in any given method; give each method an adequate period of time for testing, months not days.

Cellular Wisdom at Work

 Molecules and receptors for those molecules are matched within the body, as a key that fits a lock. This universal mechanism pervades all molecules and their receptors in every cell, tissue, and organ in the body. Knowing that morphine was able to suppress pain sent researchers looking for a molecule like morphine made by the body. This led them to find the molecule endorphin, or endogenous morphine, which binds to the morphine receptor. When receptors are discovered today and the molecule binding to them unknown, we call them "orphan" receptors because we're so sure that we will eventually find the molecule that binds to that receptor.

The message of our body is that if we have a contribution there are people who are in need of receiving your contribution. The match applies to life as well as it does to molecules and their receptors.

The confidence that this is true creates a sense of safety. Even if you have not yet identified the specifics of what you will create or re-engineer in your career, profession, or business, be assured that you will find it, and that if you are on a path of a Life on Purpose there will be those who will want to receive it.

6) How will you survive financially while you get started?

Taking time with a plan to address this question will very likely spell the difference between success and failure for your dream. As John cautioned Maria,

Taking on too much financial responsibility too soon can and usually does spell disaster.

Begin with the absolute barest essential form needed to accomplish the immediate steps. You might not need a website presence on the Internet to get started. If and when you do, start simply and build it up as needed. Make sure that your website truly represents what you believe viewers will want to know about you, your product or services and how you can help them meet their needs. Find a designer who will provide you the graphics needed to print initial brochures or flyers, or if you are so inclined, develop your own. You can expand on the initial idea as demand—and especially income—grow. Do what the new circumstances require, not more.

Advertising can be very tricky. You cannot prove whether a medium will work, or not, by running trial programs. Research indicates that people must repeatedly see or hear something for at least thirteen weeks. If you purchase a minimum time you will have not adequately explored whether that medium is effective for you or not. Choose what medium you want to work with initially and stick with it for a period of time to assess its value to you.

If you don't have any cash left after paying your bills, print some flyers and business cards on your computer and start talking to people. Start with people you know, people they know, people in businesses who could benefit from your service or product, and people who are influential in their circle of friends who might like what you have to offer. There is no substitute for talking face to face, particularly people you know and telling people about your service or product. Marketing "known to known" (you are known by these people and you know them) represents the most effective marketing to date. Flyers left on door knobs of people you do not know "unknown to unknown" (you are unknown to them and they are unknown to you) will not produce sales. Business cards left on bulletin boards at grocery stores and barber shops will not produce sales. Don't rely on business cards or flyers to get your business jump-started. The best use of business cards, flyers, or brochures is to have something with your contact information on it to leave in the hands of some-one you have just talked to and who is interested in what you offer. Try craigslist.com or other free or inexpensive Internet classifieds. Schedule a meeting in your home (you don't have to offer refresh-ments), and invite three to five friends or acquaintances. Give a brief presentation of what you provide, making sure you tell them what it is that makes doing business with you unique, and what benefits they can expect.

No matter what medium you decide to try, one method or several at once, make sure you stay with them for at least a six-month period and be *sure* you have a means of tracking which method produces sales. This might be as simple as asking customers where they heard about you and making a note of it on your copy of the sales receipt. It might entail a code or key word from different media that the customer would mention in order to get a discount. The codes would tell you which medium carried the ad they saw. This is the ONLY way you can know, *proven*, which advertising methods will produce the most cash sales for you. Once you know that a method works, you can think about the advisability of a more extensive campaign, if funds are available to warrant it. Periodically review the results you are getting, because even a proven method won't necessarily be effective indefinitely.

It would have been foolish for Maria to quit her full-time job at the hardware store before she knew whether the jewelry business had an extremely good chance of supporting her. By taking a sensible, step by step approach, Maria avoided the heartache of finding herself without a job or an income. That precaution helped boost her confidence in the outcome of the experiment, and that confidence provided a step toward courage in leaving her comfort zone, *not* her means of paying her bills. Stepping without a plan in place is not courageous, it's foolhardy. The same thing applies if you are looking to change jobs or careers.

Give yourself the love and respect you deserve, and plan your steps carefully and sensibly, staying alert for new opportunities. We cannot emphasize this enough: Keep your financial bases covered in every step of your plan. The love you give yourself in this is the essence of wisdom. Have a wise plan in place and the discipline to follow the plan. You can make it less burdensome by making a game of finding creative, less expensive alternatives, watching your financial bottom line grow with each wise financial decision you make, and celebrating each milestone as it is reached. Keep in mind that you won't be able to make your contribution to the world if your idea never gets off the ground due to poor planning and execution.

When I reviewed our income and expense records for the previous twelve months before starting my coaching business, the information made certain decisions obvious to me. I would sell the condo bought with monies my mother left me when she died five years earlier. This would allow us to pay off our mortgage, reducing our monthly expenses. I weighed my needs for the coming year when my income would be greatly reduced. This process led me to conclude that my freedom to pursue a business of my own loomed larger than my need to buy additional clothes or jewelry. Raised by parents with a European lineage, wine complemented our food every evening at supper. Calculating how much we had spent on wine the previous year, which escalated as our taste and discriminatory capacity developed, I informed my husband that I would not give up wine. I wanted him to continue to purchase wine, but to considerably reduce what we spent on it. It was easy for me to make the decisions to temporarily give up these purchases or to reduce expenditures, because of the liberating freedom and joy I experienced as I conceived of and developed my own business. These spending decisions were a small price for that freedom, and they made the difference between success and failure in my early stages. They also provided me the peace of mind of knowing I would not be spreading my resources too thinly during the fragile start-up phase.

7) Keep it legal

Part of your responsibility as a business owner is to learn about all local, state, and federal laws that regulate your particular venture. If you sell a product, you will probably be required to pay local and state sales taxes, but this varies by location, so do some research. It is much less expensive in time and money over the long haul to do what is required of you from day one than it is to get embroiled in regulatory conflicts, penalties, and fines.

8) Track your progress

Keeping financial records makes sense on many levels. Good financial records will make tax preparation a breeze. If you track your income and expenses in an accounting software package, you will have easy access to reports that will tell you where every penny is going. These reports are invaluable management tools for you to see how your expenses compare to your income and whether—and where—adjustments might be in order. If you aren't inclined toward these kinds of details, hire a part-time bookkeeper to keep these records current for you. Choose someone with a good recommendation for knowledge and experience. You will be glad you did.

9) Identify and utilize effective strategies

We have discussed several strategies that have proven effective in various situations:

- What has to happen before . . .
- Recapture the joy in play at work
- Step by step—what is the simplicity beneath the complexity
- Start easy and allow it to evolve to more complex
- Scenario planning
- Create a unique position for yourself to fill a specific need in the job market
- Find and cultivate a qualified mentor
- Test the effectiveness of an advertising method; don't discard what is proven to work

10) Utilize your strengths and compensate for those areas in which you are not strong

The whole purpose of creating your strengths development plan was not to make you feel bad about the boundaries of your strengths, but rather to let you know the bases you already have covered by your strengths, and which bases you will need to plan how to cover, beyond your strengths. Once you have a solid grasp of the actual scope of your strengths, you might find that you need to fill in only here and there; or you might find that you will need a lot of good help. One is not "better" or "right." It is information to help you put your plan together with the wisdom your strengths development plan has made available. If you need information, seek it. If you need a mentor with experience and expertise in your area, look for one. If you need a steadying influence, by all means, find one. If you need help with poor thinking habits, take a workshop or two or talk with someone who has. If fear and leaving your comfort zone tend to stop you, do a minimum of one of the activities listed in Chapter 3. The more of your bases you cover in your plan, the greater are your chances for success.

The process of creating an executable plan results in clarity about specific objectives and a roadmap of ways to achieve those objectives. Jim Collins, a highly respected business consultant, author, and lecturer on the subject of company sustainability and growth reminds us that there are two ways to create a roadmap. The "paint by numbers kit in which you do what other people say, follow a well-traveled path, stay within the lines and end up with a nice, pretty—and unimaginative—picture." Or "Start with a blank canvas and try to paint a masterpiece. It is a riskier path, a harder path, a path filled with ambiguity and creative choice. But it is the only way to make your life itself a creative work of art. To paint a masterpiece requires a concept, a place to begin, a guiding context in the absence of the comforting numbers and lines in the pre-made kit. That guiding frame of reference is the highest goal."[9] You are creating your masterpiece, a creative work of art.

Cellular Wisdom at Work

 One of the amazing features of our bodies is the amount of redundancy displayed. The body employs not just one way to achieve a result but most often many, many ways. Redundancy occurs at all levels of the body. It is displayed in duplicate genes, protein processing mechanisms, neuronal pathways, signaling molecules, neurotransmitters, crosstalk between receptors, and many more. The effectiveness of redundancy is encountered as researchers "knock out" specific genes. They often find that the organism has found another way to substitute for the lacking gene by using other genes. No dysfunction is observed. Redundancy allows the molecules, cells, organs, tissues, and systems of the body to meet challenges in multiple and diverse ways to sustain the functioning of the organism.

We too can be assured that when we hit a roadblock there are ways around it. The body's teaching about redundancy suggests there is a basis for this confidence. Maybe you have yet to identify additional strategies to expand your repertoire

9   http://www.jimcollins.com/article_topics/articles/the-highest-goal.html.

and form the basis to respond creatively to perceived blind alleys. It may be helpful to expand your explorations and build a substantial framework of effective strategies essential to the success of your career, profession, or business.

Message to the Reader

Typically the process of identifying your dream and developing it does not progress linearly, but consists of stops and starts, detours and corrections, doing and being. Sluggish movement gives way to startling insight, opening doors, and unprecedented connections. Expect the waxing and waning, they are part of the process. Segments vary in length and in their significance. Expecting progress in a straight trajectory sets up unrealistic expectations and can lead to significant disappointment. Realize the path may trace a circuitous route in spite of the best-laid plans. Having a plan does not mean you won't learn new ideas along the way or modify your movement toward your dream.

Consider the extensive, holistic nature of this process of creating or recreating your dream, which involves many deep shifts in perspectives, internal and external shifts in what's important to you now in how you experience the world, and a major shift in or loss of your personal and professional identities. As we seek work that is meaningful, value driven, engaging, we give up older ideas of success as well as perceived identity to forge new ones with a different, higher, set of expectations.

This time of transition contains immense value. This is the time to shed the influences of others and delve deep into the essence of who you are and the dream you want to realize. Along the way you may experience unexpected twists and turns which might cause you to doubt your potential to realize your dream and wonder if, after all, is it possible to get there. The energy to navigate the twists and turns flows from your expectations of what your life will be like as you live a meaningful, Purposeful Life, making your contribution to the world—your vision and your dream. The famous artist Pablo Picasso tells us "Our goals can only be reached through the vehicle of a plan, in which we fervently believe, and upon which we vigorously act. There is no other route to success." Your plan, created in wisdom, will bring you back repeatedly to the next step.

Logic is great, and it most certainly has its place, but be aware that it can only take us so far. Logic and rational thinking cannot comprehend that which lies beyond their boundaries. Logic stops short of trusting the expansive and creative nature of the inner landscape. Logic stops short of accepting our unique expression of life in the world. Logic stops short of a single individual being important in the overall scheme of things. Logic stops short of intuitive impulse. Logic stops short of the serendipitous opportunity that could propel us past an entire flight of steps, and . . .

One should never be so invested in a plan that such opportunity would be lost in favor of sticking implicitly to the plan.

This has largely been a chapter about steps, but logic alone cannot meet the challenges of a world in crisis. As Albert Einstein said, "The world will not evolve past its current state of crisis by using the same thinking that created the situation."

The challenges currently facing the world economic system are exemplary of the failure of old patterns and systems to keep pace with an evolving world. When one aligns with inner resources and a Life on Purpose, the condition of the exterior world becomes much less relevant. The crumbling of an old system is no longer a major factor, because of the power in that with which we choose to align, and the new story which we are choosing to write.

Where we want to go will require the wisdom of coupling logic with the alignment of our thoughts, our actions, our dreams, and our inner selves. This is the next dimension—the next step—of the evolution of our story.

Alan Lakein, an author on the subject of time management, said, "Planning is bringing the future into the present so that you can do something about it now." As individuals begin to combine sound logic with alignment, working from an old job into a dream for a new future, the story and evolution of the larger world will begin to nudge toward a new direction and form. Putting our plans into action will set the ripples in motion, beginning with the people who will want to join us in our endeavors.

||||||||||||||||||||||||||||||||||||||||||||||||||||||||||||||||||||||||||||||||||||||||||||||||||||

Intent into Action
Tools from Chapter 4: A Wise Plan

||||||||||||||||||||||||||||||||||||||||||||||||||||||||||||||||||||||||||||||||||||||||||||||||||||

Now that you have a sense of the general direction of your Purpose, a dream in the form of a statement, a vision of you living your dream, and a strengths development plan, you know where you are starting from and where you want to go. You are also hard at work developing strengths. You are now in a strong position to begin developing your plan. Planning helps you to never be at loss as to what to do next. It gives you a roadmap to follow toward your destination. It shows you the next step. A plan is never cast in stone: unexpected events or circumstances can occur, you can learn something you had not taken into consideration originally, an opportunity might arise that you decide to pursue that will require altering the planned route. Don't abandon your plan frivolously, but don't be rigidly bound to an inflexible plan either. Navigate by your dream, your vision, your mission statement, and your West. Your plan is simply a tool to help you get there.

Planning entails converting your overall goal into small enough steps that you can begin following the directives of the plan toward the realization of your dream. The easiest way to do this is to decide where you want to be relative to your dream at some future time. There will be the big steps that need to happen in order to get there. Let's refer again to our dog lover. Suppose you decide that you want to have all of your elements in place within five years: classes, lectures and workshops, clubs, and board games—that create new opportunities for the expression of love for dogs. You would take those elements, the biggest steps, and plan to add one new element every few months. This gives you time to develop each element. Remember, however, to stay alert to opportunities.

You may not be a person who can possibly determine what needs to be accomplished each week or make daily TO DO lists for that week's tasks. Instead, you may want to envision reaching overall goals—what you need to accomplish.

Be sure to include in your plan the roles needed to be filled on your team. Check out legal requirements for engaging in your activity and abide by them. Provide a means for tracking your income, expenditures, and marketing effectiveness as well as your progress toward your goal. And absolutely be sure to plan carefully for how you will survive financially every step of the way.

The planning process does not need to use more logic and left-brain thinking than the previous steps!

A *wise* plan allows for the unexpected and still keep your bases covered.

- *Take the next step: break your goals into future-based tasks.*

- *Plan for building your team, for your finances along the way, for what is required by local and state authorities, and for how you will reach and retain your ideal customers.*

- *Use the plan as a roadmap, but NOT as a rigid constrictor; reevaluate priorities and timing and allow for unexpected opportunities as you go.*

5

Committed People: Your Team

Never doubt that a small group of thoughtful, committed people
can change the world. Indeed. It is the only thing that ever has.

—MARGARET MEAD

Wisdom from Your Strengths Development Plan

By this stage of our journey together you will have a good idea of your dream, your vision
for it, a good grasp of your strengths and your strengths development plan, and at least
the beginnings of a plan based on the wisdom of giving yourself the best possible shot at
success. You know the general categories of people you will need to help you at different
stages of the development and expansion of your dream. Now it is time to discuss more
specifically who you would want to choose to fill the various roles you have identified. It
doesn't matter what your particular transition or project is—seeking a promotion, changing
jobs, changing careers, starting or expanding a business of your own, or seeking someone

with a compatible dream to offer you support—the principles of building a supportive team or being part of a supportive team of committed people is the same.

Approach this with thoughtfulness and care. As you progress from a single individual, you, to a team effort, the strengths approach expands to encompass the entire group.

The strengths of the individuals you choose will shape the effectiveness of the collective team you create.

If you choose your best friend because you've known her since second grade and she needs a job, that's well and good, but does she also add valuable strengths to your effort? Is there a specific role for which she is ideally suited and is that role needed right now, or are you simply doing your friend a favor so she will think well of you? You can save yourself and your friend future headaches and hard feelings by taking this into account from day one. It is far more difficult to fire a friend than to not hire her in the first place, if she will not add significantly to your effort. It can be fatal to your venture to carry someone along who doesn't really contribute because you don't have the heart to tell them *No*.

The people who will add the most to your venture or transition are those with personal strengths that, in addition to having the skill sets needed, specifically complement your strengths, whether it is knowledge and experience in a certain area, clean and positive thinking habits and beliefs, emotional maturity, or good character.

Stories

Author's Story

Every Sunday my father and his seven brothers sat at the table after lunch, talking about the challenges and opportunities they encountered in their businesses. Each had left the country family truck farm in Dalcour, LA, to move to New Orleans and establish their grocery stores. For hours they strategized. They compared cash flow; shared fiscal concerns; explored each other's ideas extensively, including each one's perspective about what was necessary to effectively run a profitable business. They discussed how, when, and what actions to pursue to further develop their businesses, what strategies were proving effective for each, including upcoming trends, concerns for the future, and what they thought about offering credit to their customers.

Listening from afar, intrigued by their enthusiasm, I witnessed these conversations every Sunday afternoon for years as a child. Beginning my new life phase as a coach, starting up a small business, I found myself doubting, questioning. What did I know about starting and running a business? Well, for one thing I knew my father's corner grocery store. As a child, I sat behind the cash register every afternoon after school. Every Sunday I listened to my father and my uncle's conversations. As I remembered these discussions, I began to realize I had been given an apprenticeship in the business of relationships, goods, prices, processes, and values by my family. The experience of listening to talk about my father's dreams with his brothers around the Sunday dinner table has stayed with me. He showed me how to dream. He and my uncles let me see the value of support in business as they shared ideas and resources over lengthy Sunday lunches.

Initially, I had not thought these experiences relevant to my transition out of academia to start up a small business. But, as the idea of my own coaching business took hold and collaborators began to appear, I realized that like my father and uncles, I too could benefit enormously from interacting with a group of supporters. Alone, I possessed only my own knowledge and skills and could perceive only some of the issues that might face me as I developed a business. If I was surrounded by those who cared about me and whom I trusted, like my father with his brothers, I would have a team to support me, to provide the expertise I alone could not bring to the table. To be successful I would need to assemble a team—trusted business relationships would be essential to building the foundation of my vision.

Committed People: Jacob (J.B.) Schramm   *Stories*

Jacob (J.B.) Schramm grew up in Denver, Colorado, attending inner city schools with friends of varying economic and ethnic backgrounds. In *How to Change the World: Social Entrepreneurs and the Power of New Ideas,*[10] Jacob Schramm, a champion of change, writes, "I went from elementary to junior high and from junior high to high school

---

[10] Schramm, J. B. 2004. The Talent is Out There. In *How to Change the World: Social Entrepreneurs and the Power of New Ideas,* edited by Bornstein, David.

with the same group of guys . . . We all had our strengths. And I just assumed that we'd all go on to the next stage in life together. College was a given . . . When I found out that a lot of them weren't going, it was a jolt. It lodged in me. It profoundly didn't make sense. And the difference was not that they were less college capable than I was." His awareness of the lives of youngsters with limited opportunity emerged again when J.B. volunteered for a summer camp, run by an African American Episcopal Church, for young people in trouble with the law.

While at Harvard Divinity School, Schramm took a job as a freshman academic advisor to help to pay his way. Reviewing the admission files of newly enrolled students, he often noticed the comment, "Wish we could find ten more like him," scribbled in the margins of applications from low-income students. Schramm decided not to become ordained upon graduating Harvard, but joined a non-profit organization that ran a teen center located in a low-income housing complex, the Jubilee Housing Development. Here he created the Flyers Tutoring Program where students would be helped with their homework by a tutor three nights a week. At the end of the school year, they would have the opportunity to participate in an outdoor youth program in Colorado or Florida. While he witnessed low income students with top grades and high test scores successfully apply to and enter college, the vast major-ity of students with average grades and test scores would not enter college. He realized that many of these students had accomplished other things, such as writing screen plays or other artistic, social, or political endeavors. However, these accomplishments never made it into the pages of their college applications. He wanted the colleges to see these youngsters as he did.

Four students with lots of potential but only average grades and SAT scores approached Schramm for help getting into college in 1993. He wrestled with the challenge of how to convey their poten-tial. He ". . . had faith that if they . . . told a part of their story that was important to them [in a heartfelt essay], it would convey their strengths to another human being in a way that nothing else could." Schramm enlisted a small team to start: Keith Frome, his closest friend and the best writing teacher he knew from graduate school, and Derek Canty, a youth motivator who had a gift for teenagers to see each other as one another's coaches, not critics. With this team, Schramm started College Summit. The four students applied to college with the help of Schramm and his team. Two were accepted and attended Brown University and Montgomery County Community College, and two received full scholarships to Connecticut College in New London, CT.

A strategy essential to College Summit's success is the training of students who are influential within their high schools, capable of influencing their peers and building a college-going culture. More than 7,000 influential students have been trained since 1993. While their high school GPA is 2.9 on a 4.0 scale, their college enrollment (78%) is significantly above the national college enrollment rate of low-income students (46%). Further, the retention rate for these students has been eighty percent, far above the national rate of all college students.

College Summit reports significant success in attaining their goals.[11] Together with its partner high schools, College Summit served students in California, Colorado, Missouri, West Virginia, the District of Columbia, Maryland, Virginia, South Carolina, North Carolina, Wisconsin, and New York in the 2006–2007 school year. Growth in terms of the number of students served at Summit partner schools culminated at a 2008–2009 level of 16,800 seniors, a forty percent average annual increase. In addition, 1,600 teachers and counselors have been trained to serve 40,000 students, including Summit's continuing support services provided throughout the school year. Finally, a fifty-one percent increase has occurred in the number of partner schools since 2005.

Schramm's team of committed, support people started small and grew to include:

- Keith Frome, best writing teacher in the area
- Derek Canty, youth motivator who helped teens become each other's coaches, not critics

---

[11] *www.collegesummit.org.*

- 40,000 high school students in partner schools trained to influence peers and build a college-going culture
- 1,600 teachers and counselors, who serve the 40,000 students

Committed People: John Wood

A specialist in international markets, John Wood led Microsoft's expansion into Asia during a period of bombastic growth in the technology industry in the 1990s. After working at Microsoft for seven years with seventy-five people reporting to him, John took a much needed break and visited Nepal in 1998 for twenty-one days of trekking the Annapurna circuit in the Himalayas. Exhausted from overwork, he was plagued by the question: "Is this all there is—longer hours and bigger payoffs?" He secretly harbored a desire to do something lasting and significant. As he watched a presentation of trekking in Nepal offered by a local adventure travel company, John was awed by the majestic images of the mountains. Not long after that, he began his adventure walking over 200 miles of donkey trails with all his gear in his backpack. An unseen change in his life and work was about to occur when John struck up a conversation with Pasupathi, a friendly middle aged Nepali man wearing thick glasses sitting at an adjacent table in the trekker's lodge. Asking what he did for a living, Pasupathi answered, "District resource person for Lamjung Province." He explained that he was responsible for finding resources, including books, for seventeen rural schools in Nepal. Pasupathi told John that the children are eager to learn, but, "We do have not enough schools. We do not have sufficient school supplies. Everyone is so poor we cannot make much investment in education." John asked Pasupathi question after question, eager to learn more. The conversation drew John into Pasupathi's world. John asked where he was headed next. "He was leaving in the morning to visit a school in the village of Bahundanda. It was a three-hour walk up steep hills." John asked if he could join him. It was the second day of his trek. In his book, John describes reaching the school and watching the children "clad in uniforms of dark blue pants and powder blue shirts, [as they] ran by us as a clanking bell signaled the start of the school day."[12] They smiled at the foreign visitor as they scrambled to enter their school.

Walking into the school library John was shocked. There were no desks, no chairs, no shelves, and no books. He asked the headmaster, "Where are the books?" A summoned teacher brought the key to a rusty padlock and opened the cabinet. A Danielle Steele romance novel, a novel written in Italian, and other castoffs of backpackers peppered the shelves of the cabinet. The books hardly contributed to the education of the 450 students in the school. John was amazed and disappointed. As John was leaving the library, the headmaster made a comment that would prove to have a profound effect on John's life and work. "Perhaps, Sir, you will someday come back with books."

A lover of reading as a child, John could not fathom educating children with no books. Invited to tea, the teachers made a fervent plea for books. After visiting the rural school, John returned to Kathmandu, the capital and the largest city in Nepal, stopped at an Internet cafe, opened his computer, and wrote an e-mail to the 100 plus people stored in his address book making a sales pitch for people to either send books suitable for children learning English or forward the e-mail to others. "You may have books your children have outgrown and/or if you can stick a $5 bill or a $100 bill in an envelope and send it along." He promised to buy children's books in bulk with the money. His parents contacted him to inform him that his book drive resulted in 3,000 books sent to his parent's home in Denver, Colorado, and requested that he come home and sort through them and ship the books to Nepal.

A few months later John and his dad, who had asked to join him, returned to Nepal and transported the books to the rural school on the backs of donkeys. The books had arrived. The children formed a human corridor through which they walked. The headmaster made a speech telling the school children and teachers that now they had a "library full of books." Back in the city, Kathmandu, John struggled

---

[12] Wood, John. 2006. *Leaving Microsoft to Change the World: An Entrepreneur's Odyssey to Educate the World's Children.* New York: HarperCollins Publishers.

with a dilemma. In two days he was scheduled to assume a new role running business development for Microsoft's Greater China Region. He asked himself, "Did it really matter how many copies of Windows we sold in Taiwan this month when millions of children were without access to books?" A voice inside asked him, "Are there thousands lining up to help poor villages build schools and libraries? That job is not being done. You should rise to this challenge."

He would not only leave Microsoft, but he would sever ties with his girlfriend, other friends, and China. Leaving Beijing, John felt the pressures of Microsoft falling away. His decision had "finally been crystallized, been announced, and been implemented." John had viewed his education projects as a hobby, not a vocation. Having no idea of how to start, he spoke with a college friend, Jim, an experienced philanthropist who sat on the board of his family's foundation, who convinced John he must have 501(c) status to encourage donators to give. Calling an attorney, John set up his nonprofit and his friend and his wife donated $10, 000. The money was used to hire young Nepalese men to work full time on the project. A friend, Dinesh, from the Lions Club in Kathmandu, agreed to hire and manage the new employees.

Seeking funds, John came upon the Draper Richards foundation, which sought organizations in their infancy and, if the applicant was selected, would supply $100,000 per year of unrestricted funds. They were, indeed, a potential dream investor. Bill and Jenny Draper visited John's new cramped offices in San Francisco to meet John and review his proposal. Aware that he had no coherent document detailing the expansion of his education project, John stayed up all night to create a business plan. In their meeting the next day, Bill drilled John on what made him an entrepreneur. He liked what he heard and saw, including John's bright yellow North Face sleeping bag, which he spotted in the corner. John explained, "On some nights . . . this is my home." Two weeks later, John was approved as the second Draper Richards Fellow. With a three-year pledge of $100,000 per year, Room to Read was on its way.

As he was considering his desire to go global, to expand first into Cambodia and Vietnam, John received a phone call. Erin introduced herself. She was calling because a mutual friend had mentioned his work in Nepal and his desire to expand into Vietnam. Erin had a passion to help children. She had experience in Vietnam and was willing to volunteer her services. Within weeks, Erin plunged into her role and acquired donations totaling $80,000 for Room to Read in Vietnam within months. Over time, John built a team of volunteers, with a director in India. The size of the global team doubled. John had learned at Microsoft to hire smart people with strong work ethics, give them bold and specific goals, and stay out of their way. Some were corporate refugees. All believed that in Room to Read they had found "a lever with which to move the earth."

Room to Read's long-term goal is "to build 20,000 schools and libraries, educating 10 million children in the developing world by 2020."[13] In less than ten years, Room to Read has set up operations in Nepal, Vietnam, Cambodia, India, Sri Lanka, Laos, South Africa, Zambia, and Bangladesh; it has built 765 schools, serving 210,000 students, built 7,048 libraries, and has published 310 original titles in local languages.

Their successful approach to the problem of rural education involves finding committed people to help in:

- Partnering with communities to build schools through their challenge grant program
- Establishing bilingual libraries
- Publishing local language children's books
- Establishing computer and language labs
- Providing long-term scholarships to girls

In a recent interview John proclaimed, "The human spirit and this amazing device called the brain will allow people to break the cycle of poverty, within one generation, if kids grow up with books and schools. In the greatest era of wealth creation in human history, can't we reach deep, and give those kids that amazing opportunity?"[14]

---

[13] *www.roomtoread.org.*
[14] Wood, John. It Began With Books. On *Microsoft, Meaning, and the Drive to Help Educate Children Across the Developing World. Newsweek,* 2008.

John's inspiring commitment to his dream eventually led him to a team consisting of:

- Pasupathi, early inspiration and advisor who opened John's eyes to a need
- John's parents, who helped manage the initial influx of books
- Jim, friend and advisor who recommended setting up a legal non-profit for receiving donations
- An attorney, who helped set up the non-profit organization
- Dinesh, who hired and managed new employees in Kathmandu
- Bill and Jenny Draper, who provided funding
- Erin, who volunteered to help with fundraising in the expansion into Cambodia and Vietnam
- The director in India
- The unnamed hundreds of volunteers and employees who eventually helped run the project around the world.

Message to the Reader

Let's think about these inspiring stories in the context of what we have learned so far. Did you notice how my family influence was a large factor in shaping and educating me for my Purposeful dream, just like we talked about in Chapter 2? And did you also notice that upon reflection, I found that I possessed more strengths in the area of running a business than I first thought? I absorbed those as a child, long before I knew their value or dreamed of recalling or relying on them. And did you notice that my father and uncles all supported each other in compatible dreams of running successful grocery stores?

Did you notice how J. B. Schramm and John Wood each discovered his Purpose in stages as his vision grew, very similar to Greg Mortenson's, building schools in remote rural Pakistan and Afghanistan? They all started with a small idea, a step they thought they could accomplish, and allowed the venture to evolve into something much more complex than they first imagined. This process is organic in that it reflects how organisms begin as single cells and later transition into more complex structures.

Schramm identified and recruited the members to his team that he needed to help him not only increase the number of low-income students applying for college, but to recognize their strengths and present their applications in a way that would allow the colleges to see the potential of average students. He brought aboard individuals with specific expertise, trained student influencers, and partnered with high schools to catapult the initiative to success.

Neither Schramm nor Wood nor Mortenson set out to build gigantic organizations. Their motivation came from their visions of giving better opportunities for growth to individuals with limited support resources. They offered something that those who observed their efforts wanted for themselves, and their services came to be in great demand because of the value of and need for the *service,* not due to the business ambition or expertise of the founders. As the demand grew, each of these individuals attracted others who wanted to be part of their dream in support of the growing effort. This illustrates how:

One person, Living on Purpose, attracts others who recognize and resonate with a vision larger than the individuals involved and who want to contribute in an environment of living a larger life.

Did you notice how John Wood first thought about his interest in providing books to the children in Nepal? He thought of reading as a hobby, not as a vocation, an example of the dream growing from a personal interest. Often, we fail to recognize that our hobbies frequently harbor the essence of our dreams. We minimize their importance and fail to see the relationship to our Purpose. What we miss in this kind of thinking is often our best gifts, passing them off as "only hobbies." Interests and talents are inextricably woven into the fabric of our Life's Purpose and often offer some of our best opportunities for expressing ourselves and expanding into our outer world.

Erin was invaluable in the unfolding of John's dream. She heard about John's work and wanted to be part of it in whatever way she could. She took the initiative and contacted John to offer her services. She had knowledge of the needs in Vietnam, John's next area of focus. She was an effective fundraiser. She was a team member made in heaven in how perfectly she filled the need at exactly the right time. Erin's assets provided just the knowledge and expertise he needed for his next steps. This is the kind of synchronistic connection that

Living on Purpose often provides. When you follow a dream with integrity—alignment—from the core of your being, as John found himself doing, you are Living on Purpose, and a whole new universe of possibilities presents itself.

John would not have had the impact on education in the nine countries Room to Read operates in without recognizing his dream, his Purpose, and employing a strong team to deliver it. Whatever the stage of development of your business, career, or profession, you will benefit from formulating a team of committed people who is effective in helping you further develop your dream, your unique work.

Cellular Wisdom at Work

Repeated patterns of interdependence are displayed in the body every moment. This interdependence between cells, organs, and systems underlies the wide repertoire of actions that we as humans typically embody. Cells were required to specialize—focus on the development of specific capacities—to make possible the emergence of multi-cellular organisms. No longer were individual cells required to perform all necessary functions: digestion, movement, reproduction. With specialization, muscle cells developed the capacity to contract and expand. Red blood cells developed the capacity to carry and distribute nutrients. Neurons developed the capacity to conduct and communicate electrical and chemical signals. Each cell type brings a unique capacity to the body.

Since individual cells no longer performed all required functions, it was necessary for specialized cells to cooperate fully and integrate their actions to give rise to multi-cellular organizations. A harmonious synergy between cells, organs and systems, each with their specific functions, leads to very precise and orchestrated activities which occur in our bodies every moment. These mechanisms of cooperation and integration of function allow us to move, sit, walk, or talk. Synergy of function makes possible the wide range of activities that characterizes us as humans.

Although we may not comprehend all the elements that will catapult our inner dream into outer reality, we can appreciate that synchronistic events will occur to help us orchestrate the emergence of our dream into the outer world. This expectation forms the foundation of our interdependence on other resources, people, places, events, and opportunities. Exquisitely poised to recognize these opportunities, we stand on the brink of realizing our dreams and beyond.

The message broadcast by every molecule, cell, organ, and system in the body calls to us to understand that we do not do it alone. Our cells naturally reach out to each other. We have the option of listening to this inherent wisdom and reaching out for or denying what others might offer us. J. B. Schramm, John Wood, my father and uncles, Greg Mortenson, Joe Jaworski, Bill Strickland, or Catherine Rohr could not have accomplished what they have each accomplished by themselves. All of these stories illustrates the potential of what a team of committed people can do.

Message to the Reader

> *The multidimensional aspect of interacting with others brings us perspectives grander than those we normally employ, opportunities we may not have recognized or envisioned, and insights about the convergence of talents and skills that might have escaped our watchful awareness.*

As social creatures, we live together and influence each other continually. Nonetheless, when it comes to realizing our dream work, career, or business endeavor, we may mistakenly feel as though to be a winner we must do it alone. Understand that realizing our dream, while requiring personal focus and energy, does not require us to have all we need to create it alone. Reaching out to others is an expression of our social being, as easy and natural as the relationship between bones, muscles, and nerves.

Perhaps you are not starting a new enterprise, perhaps you are looking for a new job opportunity wherein you might pursue your own dreams of making an important contribution by bringing your expertise to help develop the dream of someone else. In that case, your "team" might come in the form of a mentor who has contacts in the field you hope to transition into, or a career coach whom you hire on an hourly basis to help you line up your strengths in the most favorable light and who might offer invaluable insight into your idea, or the career counselor at your local college or job center who might help you learn to interview more effectively or evaluate the educational requirements of that new position, or an agent at an employment agency who helps match you up with potential employers, or a combination of these. Your best friend might introduce you to someone who knows someone else developing a dream you would like to support, or a coworker might offer a bit of wisdom you had not thought of. No matter your specific objective, the network of people around you can help you realize that objective in ways you could not have done on your own.

While you may be familiar with the value of teams in large corporations, particularly multinational companies, you may not yet appreciate the positive impact of teams in smaller projects. As a solopreneur, solo—running your business single-handedly, maybe with contractors for hire, yet with full responsibility for the running of your business,[15] most of your team is likely to not be in-house but utilized in a one-on-one basis, in small groups or contracted for specific tasks. Because your dream and your needs are unique, the team you develop will likely look extraordinarily different than that of another entrepreneur or professional. Consider the important interactions you might need to have, or already have, with team members such as your accountant as tax time approaches, your printer as deadlines loom, your marketing person as you prepare for a trade show or presentation, your computer consultant as you meet technical challenges, most often the night before a deadline.

Though I am a solopreneur who basically works alone, I benefit enormously from interacting with what I fondly refer to as my "executive team." Initially, my team included a lawyer and a tax accountant. Today my team includes a marketing consultant, publicist, publisher, tax accountant, QuickBooks accountant, financial planner, lawyer, bank advisor, printer, graphics and web designer, web coder, web host, affiliated coaches, and a psychiatrist with whom I collaborate in a second business, Transition Pathways.

---

[15] *www.urbandictionary.com.*

Researchers point out, "A single focus creates blind spots that prevent it [the business] from exploring new 'blue oceans' of market opportunities that may exist."[16] The members of your team provide a diverse perspective beyond your focus in addition to assisting you in the many day to day decisions you must make in your business. They help create an awareness of what is occurring or might occur. Research (cited above) reinforces that, "at the individual level, people tend to force the world to fit their existing cognitive frames: there is a built-in self-reinforcing tendency to shoehorn what is observed into current dominant schemes of perception and cognition." This emphasizes the need for peripheral awareness beyond your dominant habits of looking at the world, which can be provided by a team of thoughtfully selected individuals committed to your vision. The right team can help you move past some of your blind spots and some of your habitual limited thinking.

Adding diverse perspectives is one strength you will not encounter if there is only one of you on your team, but by thoughtfully choosing individuals to help you, you can add a new component to your strengths development plan. The same thing applies to helping minimize your own blind spots; this strength only available in team situations, directly addresses a need you may not have even known you had.

Often, there are individuals already around us who might be waiting in the wings for a chance to join forces on our dreams, people we know, people who would be delighted to combine their assets and dreams with ours. This is a valuable resource worth tapping as long as we use common sense about the actual usefulness of each individual. And we may already have a small team in place, but never thought of the accountant or print shop owner as part of our "team." This little shift in perspective can make a difference in how we interact with these people and how we move forward in developing our dreams.

---

[16] Pina e Cunha, Miguel and Robert Chia. 2007. Using Teams to Avoid Peripheral Blindness. *Long Range Planning* 40, no. 6:559–573.

Whatever form your transition takes, recognize the value of a team of committed people to provide creative, insightful perspectives through innovative interactions to help you make high quality choices. Whether you are starting a new business, transitioning from one career to another, taking on a new leadership role, entering the work place after a long absence, or developing your career, the value you can derive from working with a team of committed individuals who can support your process with diverse input is undeniable.

Cellular Wisdom at Work

 Biological organisms, larger and more complex than a single cell, require diverse cell types to carry out varied functions. Think of your own body's functions: walking, seeing, stretching, talking, digesting food, discerning odors and sounds. Smaller, less complex organisms can operate with fewer cell types. As complexity increases, functionality increases. This increase in complexity occurs in the center organism and at every level in the body— within systems, such as the nervous system, and even within single cells or genes utilized in single cells. It is reported that neurons, very complex cells, utilize much more of the DNA than any other cell types.

As you transition your life from simple types of work to more complex models, like developing a business or changing careers, your needs for a team expand to support you in effectively implementing your new plan. Like a differentiating organism, your work will most likely require an expanded repertoire of functions, served by a larger team, as the complexity of your evolving work unfolds.

Message to the Reader

The right team members will be able to perform essential functions. They will help you see around blind corners, plan for unanticipated outcomes, develop strategies aligned with your strengths, and successfully develop your business, career, or profession. You will see evidence of their support and their commitment as they appreciate your vision and goals.

Even in your role of growing leadership, you need not do it alone. You can opt to create a think tank of individuals to help you make executive decisions with the combined perspectives of a group. Whether your dream is to transition from one career to a different one, to assume a new leadership position, to start or expand a business, to go to college, or to create a non-profit venture, you could benefit greatly from developing a relationship with one or two advisors with whom to interact. You can tap into and utilize the varying perspectives, talents and strengths of others to help you develop your dream. The larger your dream, the sooner you will be likely to feel the need of adding this option, but even a small enterprise can benefit from a team of advisors.

In these chapters we have mentioned several helpful roles you might want to add to your project or transition effort that are not specifically connected with performing your service or making your product. Here we offer further suggestions for services they might provide:

- **Mentor(s):** an individual(s) who has experience and expertise in specific areas pertinent to your dream. This person will usually serve their purpose during your planning and start-up period. Their role is to teach you the things you need to know as you get started about business management and your required job skills, and to support you until you can do it without their input. You may have a series of mentors as your business/career/service unfolds.

- **Consultant or coach:** generally a hired professional who can help you learn where to best focus your energy and attention during a given period, most often transitions, of the development or realization of your dream. Their insight might help you muster the courage to break out of your habitual thinking patterns, to help you see that you have many options available, or to encourage you along your entire journey. They help you see who you are becoming as you take the steps of your journey.

- **Advisor(s):** generally one or two trusted peers with business management, marketing, or technical experience, who can help you refine your business plan, develop effective strategies, brainstorm marketing ideas, or make executive decisions. In a larger venture you might feel the need for more advisors to gain specific knowledge bases.

These roles are specifically geared toward helping you plan, start, and run your dream project or make your dream transition. You might use just one of the above or all of them, as you feel the need. These helpers can provide you with broader perspective and expanded insight based on the collective input from the group, however large or small it is.

You do not want to fill these roles with people just like you; you want to add diversity of opinion and perspective for the specific purpose of broadening your own.

No matter what roles you are looking to fill, you want to get the most supportive, most authentic and open people you can find. The optimistic attitudes of those who work with you, even if only on occasion, can provide an immense boost to you as you venture into unknown territory. The more closely aligned your dream is with theirs, the better you will be able to support each other in stressful situations.

Filling a Role Creatively

Let's examine the specific steps you can take to help ensure that you bring on board committed individuals who are best qualified and the best fit for your operation:

1) Identify the role to be filled and how soon it needs to be filled. A detailed job description will define exactly what will be expected. It is not good business to have someone start to work expecting to do one thing, only to have you continually adding to the list without additional compensation. Think carefully about this ahead of time. Be prepared to pay more when more tasks or responsibilities are added.

2) Create a list of individuals who are interested, either as a result of personal networking or from a help wanted ad.

3) Assess their suitability for the role:
   - Personal competency—do they have the education, experience, skills, and willingness to do the job needed?
   - Personal strengths—will their strengths complement yours and vice versa?
   - Personality profile—is their personality suited to the particular job?
   - Similarity or compatibility of vision and dreams—will they feel like your vision and dream is part of their own? Shared visions and dreams can form particularly strong bonds of mutual loyalties.

4) Make a decision from the wisdom of all the valuable information you now have; resist the temptation to make a decision from emotional attachment.

5) Use the same wisdom in hiring that Maria used when she created her successful plan for the transition from her cashier job to entrepreneur.

> *You don't have to have a lot of financial resources available to bring someone on board.*

6) Compensate people for their contributions. An equitable exchange of energy is important. Compensate your team members adequately for their invaluable contributions to the realization of your dream. Their compensation might be in a form other than an hourly wage or salary:

   - Experience to add to their resume
   - Use of your computer or specialized equipment in their off hours in exchange for their time
   - Teach them a new skill
   - Help them with an aspect of their dream in exchange for their work on yours
   - Pay them a small percentage of your collected net sales
   - A combination from above in lieu of a portion of their wage

The possibilities are endless. If you can find something other than cash that the individual needs or can benefit from, you might be able to earn their services rather than pay them. Make the terms beneficial and agreeable to *both* parties and clearly define the exchange in writing to clarify what is expected.

Once you constitute your team, show appreciation for what they do. Recognize their value and their contribution. Outline a plan with certain benchmarks (goals) that will be rewarded: a raise, a promotion, a bonus, a class or seminar. When a benchmark is reached, follow up with their reward. Whenever possible, give a bonus that was unexpected for a job particularly well done. This will engender trust. Find ways to help them expand and grow in your process together. This is win-win at its best.

7) Represent your needs and what you can afford to pay. A mutually beneficial fit is what you seek, not something that only benefits one side of the table. Explore every advantage possible wherein you both can gain what you want and need.

For those of you who are looking to change careers or jobs, not start a company of your own, these remain important principles for you. If you know the kinds of things a prospective employer is looking for, their needs, if you have your personal strengths development plan filled out thoughtfully and know your competency and have confidence in your authentic abilities and inner resources and believe you can contribute to their venture, you will go into every interview with a decided advantage over the next applicant. Remember, you are looking for a *mutually beneficial fit*. Seek the kind of situation where you can grow personally and bring your own dream into the company you will work for.

If you find you have made an error in your selection of an individual, terminate the relationship as soon as possible. Keeping a negative influence on board will undermine your progress and your resources. How do you know if someone needs to go? The following are some of the most common signs:

- Repeated failure to deliver a task as specified
- Lack of interest in the vision and the team effort
- Inability to communicate constructively to the team

If you observe these behaviors, reflect on your own behavior to make sure that you have done your part. If you suspect you have not, correct your oversight before taking corrective action with a team member; otherwise, you may have a repeating situation. You don't want to let someone go who is dealing with something you could have taken care of yourself. Do not blame an employee or colleague for something you did or failed to do.

- Have I made my expectations clear and are they reasonable?
- Have I provided appropriate training and descriptions of exactly what is expected?
- Have I clearly communicated the vision, and do I repeat it often?
- Have I asked for input from this individual on what they perceive the specific challenge is?
- Have I listened to their responses and weighed the validity of their concerns?
- Once I have done all that I need to do, if the behavior still continues, have I told them that their behavior is not acceptable and, if continued, could lead to termination?

Following these steps can minimize those unfortunate situations that arise occasionally in business environments. Keep your emotions under your control. Use tact when you find that you must let someone go.

The Challenges of Diversity

As projects and teams expand, an interesting phenomenon begins to emerge in the dynamics of the work environment. Each person adds his or her unique set of skills, talents, education, knowledge, and perspective. This wonderful diversity is the stuff from which great teams are built, because what one team member may lack, another is likely to offer. This same diversity can also create some of the greatest challenges. In addition to all the contributions the individuals pool together in the team effort, they also co-mingle their fears, prejudices, habits and personality quirks, areas of immaturity, and foibles. Coordinating and balancing these diverse elements requires thoughtfulness, tact, and leadership. As your project becomes more complex, requiring a larger team with a greater range of skills, your role as leader and motivator becomes greater. As your dream expands, your contribution will also expand and evolve. This expansion is what gives new life to your dream and new awareness, joy, and meaning to you and to your team members as you encourage their expansion and evolution.

What makes a team effective? Commitment to a common goal constitutes the cohesive glue that brings a diverse team together. The group dynamics of a diverse team are likely to be more complex than a more homogenous group. Potential conflict and different understandings of processes may arise. Leading a diverse team requires improved communication and consistent high quality leadership. Effective communication is one of your biggest allies in this task.

Cellular Wisdom at Work

Every cell and system in our body continually communicates with other cells and systems, providing feedback regarding function. There is no moment in time when this is not occurring. Feedback mechanisms employ various strategies. Some communication, such as that provided by the blood supply, is widely distributed to all cells and tissues. Other communication, such as between neurons or between neurons and muscles, is limited to targeted cells and tissues with specific receptors or to those within close proximity.

Following the examples of our cells, tissues, and systems, communicating effectively requires us to employ varied and multiple modes of communication. This challenge invites you to stretch the ways you express yourself, requiring you to communicate both more clearly and using multiple different modes. Furthermore, this level of communication requires that you understand the expression of others from different cultures and backgrounds. Investing time and care in becoming aware of how you best communicate with all the members of your team, learning how they best communicate with you and with each other, establishes the foundation to counteract potential conflicts that might emerge.

When communication flows easily between you and the team and among team members, information shared openly and individuals respected, you know that you have created a culture that promotes interchange and integration and one in which team members can easily employ their preferred methods of communicating. You have created a highly functioning team.

Misunderstandings and conflict of opinion, interest, or style are bound to arise with(in) a diversity of individuals. Frequently the root of misunderstandings comes from differences in personality and communication types. Fortunately, there are myriad assessments available to categorize and qualify personality traits. These can be everything from very enlightening to merely entertaining. Understanding how your personality affects your interpersonal communications and your work performance can be invaluable. Some of these tests help you understand your preferable styles of approaching work and interpersonal situations.

In the well-known Myers-Briggs communication style system you recognize that if you are introverted, you are recharged by a quiet, individual activity like reading. If you are extraverted, you are energized by a social gathering. Introverts tend to think internally; extraverts tend to think verbally. Knowing this can help you understand why others might consider you to be stand-offish and aloof, when in fact you are simply processing information internally before responding to a question. Or you will better understand why others, the introverted ones, get impatient when you seem to chatter on and on, when you are simply processing out loud. This is a sample of the insight one can gain from Myers-Briggs profiling, but a useful one.

Message to the Reader

When you understand your communication and performance style and those of your team members, you will be armed with deeper insight into how people interact with each other and better prepared to lead your growing team with wisdom.

The DiSC system of personality type profiling was developed by John Geier, Ph.D. (1934–2009), a pioneer in human assessment who researched work behavioral competencies for over forty years. With the DiSC system, the basic classifications are: Dominant, Influencing, Steady, or Conscientious. Dominants, "D's," tend to delegate, make decisions, and get straight to the point or the bottom line. They get impatient with chitchat or too many details. Influencers, "I's," tend to bring people together, socialize, and use their charm. They need to feel accepted. Steadys, "S's," are the ones who are dependable, stable, and get the job done. They resist change unless they have time to get used to it. And Conscientious ones, "C's," are detail-oriented, precise, cautious, and perfectionists. They need to have all the details prior to making a decision. Most people find when they are profiled that they have one primary style with one or two others that are also influential in their behavior, making a fascinating mix of tendencies.

In communicating with these types, chat for at least a moment or two before getting to business with extraverted and "I" types. Give them details in writing and public recognition whenever appropriate. "I's" will appreciate your status. Get straight to business in your communication with "D's." Go right to the point and stick to the topic. "D" types will appreciate your competence. With "S's," use logical and systematic approaches, provide a consistent and secure environment. Give them time to adjust to changes. "S's" will appreciate your recognition of their efforts and your dependability. Communicating with "C" types give accurate and complete details, minimize socializing and emotional display. Be on time. This type will appreciate your high standards and loyalty to your team, your standards, and your vision. Allow time for introverts to think about what you have presented to them, particularly introverted "S's."

If you delegate each type with what they are best suited for, you will create harmony in your workplace, totally aside from their specific talents, experience, and knowledge bases. Recognize that over-typing individuals can minimize a person's status and contribution. The unique combinations of people's strengths may NOT follow the generalized profile. Stay attentive to people, not to their designations!

- **D**'s love tackling challenges.
- Give **I**'s freedom from control and detail.
- Count on your **S**'s to get the job done.
- Let your **C**'s analyze, organize, and control quality.

This will provide the best use of the inherent strengths in each personality on your team. Recognize your team will function more effectively with representation from each type. Each can make a specific type of contribution and bring their strength to your efforts. Knowing the types, their tendencies, their type-cast preferences, gives you an advantage in dealing with the many challenges present in a diverse community.

The assessment I use with clients is the Personal Style Profile offered by Consulting Resource Group and available on my website. It also has been researched for many years and profiles people into simpler categories: **B** profiles are action oriented and not verbal; they are impatient with talk. **A** profiles are self-expressed, good influencers, and very verbal. **I** profiles are devoted to harmony in relationships; they will not make a decision until they explore how the decision will influence everyone else. Finally, **C** profiles are devoted to data, they collect more and more data and take an incredibly long time to make a decision.

- **B**'s are action oriented.
- Give **A**'s the role of influencing others, explaining directions.
- Let your **I**'s explore the impact of all decisions on everyone involved.
- Count on your **C**'s to gather and analyze data.

Assessments are available online if you are interested in taking these as well as many others, usually for a very modest cost, or you might have an opportunity to take them in a job interview or at work. By all means do it if you are interested. Or try one of the books on the subject, such as *The 4-Dimensional Manager* by Julie Straw, Berrett-Koehler Publishers, 2002, or *The DiSC Personality System – Enhance Communication and Relationships* by Sanford Kulkin, The

Institute for Motivational Living, 2008. Information of this nature can prove invaluable on many different levels as you pursue your dream and lead your growing team.

Stories

Maria's Story

Maria is thinking hard to find ways they can have an open house showcasing her jewelry and not have to dip into her precious emergency savings. Very limited funding is her biggest challenge in moving her part-time business into its next phase. Maria and John have already decided to create only samples of the designs she wants to show, plus enough more pieces to use as door prizes to save on up-front production costs. The plan is to take orders with twenty-five percent deposits at the open house, which Maria may then use to purchase the materials she needs to make the jewelry to fill the orders. The customer will pay the balance due upon delivery of their order.

Within half an hour of concerted effort, Maria and John have produced a new budget plan that fits Maria's allotment. John volunteers to take the photos of Maria's jewelry himself, and they decide to print the brochures on Maria's computer instead of having them done professionally. They call a graphic artist John knows and he agrees to lay out the graphics for their brochure for less than his normal price. John formally volunteers his patio for the event.

Maria lets out a long sigh. It feels wonderful to see that they can still have the event and do it sensibly and within their budget, even though she has had to alter her original vision of it. It now feels solid, real, practical, and within their means. She starts to work getting the designs ready that she wants to show at the event and soon is lost in the process of designing and creating beautiful jewelry.

Everywhere she goes Maria carries a stack of brochures with her, asking people she meets on the street and in shops around town to come to her open house. Every day after getting off work at the hardware store, Maria spends an hour or two making phone calls to the officers of all the clubs and organizations she could find in her area by searching online and asking the local Chamber of Commerce. By the day of the event, she has handed out almost all of the brochures they originally printed and has had a favorable response from most of the people she has talked to. The event is a huge success.

John and Maria meet the next day to recap the results of their efforts and talk about the next steps. Maria now has over $2,000 worth of jewelry to make within the promised delivery period of three weeks. If Maria works every moment she is not at her cashier job, she would be hard pressed to produce that much that fast. They do an analysis of their production costs. If they could find someone with good dexterity and patience, who is willing to earn a set amount for each piece and who wants to work part-time to begin with, that person could help Maria meet the delivery deadline. Maria would continue to make as much of the jewelry herself as she can, saving labor costs on a portion of the production.

By Tuesday evening when John and Maria meet, there are four applicants that interest Maria. One is a housewife, Karen, who lives two blocks from Maria who wants to earn some of her own money while her kids are in school. One is a retired factory worker, Hal, who wants to do something other than watch soap operas all day. Samantha is a retired teacher whose husband died recently and who wants to take her mind off her grief. Elizabeth, the last one is a young woman who lives at home and who has Down's syndrome. Hal says he is pretty much done with dreaming, but he would like to keep busy with his hands. Samantha's dream is to help under-privileged kids have satisfying lives. Elizabeth's dream is to be part of a growing company and make an important contribution and earn her own paycheck. Karen is the only one who would not be able to start right away; she has a school play she is helping with on Thursday and Friday.

All four applicants appear willing and suitable on the surface; John and Maria rank them in descending order of suitability: Elizabeth first, Hal second, Samantha third, and Karen fourth. This ranking is mainly based on these qualifications. The position requires working alone (introverted), producing a product (**S** for getting it done, **C** for quality sensitivity).

Maria calls each candidate and tells them their decision. Samantha and Elizabeth agree to come in the next morning for a training session. They are delighted with the prospects, Elizabeth to have a real "job," and Samantha with something to meet her immediate need that could grow into something in harmony with her longer term dream. Maria now has help getting her showcase orders filled on time and the prospect of employees who will fit well with her needs both now and down the road. She is delighted with the outcome of her showcase. All signs indicate her dream will catch hold and grow, maybe beyond her wildest imagining. Things are definitely moving along.

Message to the Reader

Maria and John have given us an example of important lessons about the growing pains of a small venture with very limited financial resources. Nearly every effort faces these kinds of challenges early in development and ongoing as the enterprise grows. Using wisdom as Maria and John illustrated, will serve you all along your journey. One striking lesson from Maria's story is seeing how John, as Maria's mentor, helps keep her focused. Maria's lack of knowledge and experience running a business could be a big issue if she were trying to build her dream on her own. But with John's patience and guidance, they discover that Maria has excellent business potential with a good mind for problem solving and dreaming.

Brainstorming

There is another important tool that Maria and John used in dealing with their challenge to grow with limited funds. When they were trying to think of the possible situations where people might be willing and even happy to make $8 an hour, Maria and John "brainstormed."

Brainstorming is a strategy of letting ideas flow for the purpose of arriving at an unexpected or overlooked solution to a given problem.

A single individual can't brainstorm as effectively as a group; the momentum is derived from one person's ideas sparking new ones in someone else which sparks a new thought for another. Brainstorming can help uncover solutions when things seem to be stuck. When you can't see a solution on your own, get together with at least one other individual and let your brains storm. In an ideal world you would have one person who does nothing but write down the ideas as they come and three or more others who do nothing but come up with ideas, but it can be done with fewer participants. Here are some guidelines:

- Clearly identify the problem you need to solve.

- Write down every idea, no matter how far-fetched any of them might sound.

- Do not critique, judge, or evaluate the merits of any ideas at this time.

- Every idea has value in this process.

- If you have trouble getting the ball rolling, take a few minutes for creative play—the more laughter the better—before trying again. It can also help to have one or two ideas ready ahead of time to "prime the pump," so to speak.

- Once you have a dozen or two or three ideas written down and you know there are some good ones in the list, you can begin to evaluate which ones deserve more attention and development. Have each participant put a star by the three they can see working best for your specific solution and tell their reasons for feeling the way they do. From there, you can narrow it down to the best solution to the problem.

This is a very productive process and can be a lot of fun as well. Any time you feel stuck for a solution or a new idea, try this strategy. Many of the top corporations in the world rely on the merits of brainstorming and sometimes the best ideas come from the most surprising sources. Besides getting new ideas, this can be a great way to involve your team members in the development of the company, making them feel valued and appreciated.

In Maria's story did you notice how effective John was in keeping Maria focused on task? Left to her own devices, Maria's tendency is to let negative thoughts and limiting beliefs stop her from moving forward. John helped her over the hurdle of budgeting for the open house, and he helped keep her from getting discouraged about the prospects of a helper even before they advertised. In addition, they were very effective in bouncing ideas off each other when they needed to get their creative juices flowing. This is a functional and effective "team" at work.

Trust and Leadership

As you take on the role of leading your team with wisdom and alignment, keep individual proclivities in mind with your communication and the tasks you ask them to perform to foster an environment of trust.

Trust is the result of knowing what you can expect from someone, knowing they will uphold their end of the bargain or keep their word, knowing they will not intentionally do anything to hurt you or undermine your value.

As the leader of your evolving dream, your interactions with your team will create trust to the degree that your behavior is consistent, authentic, and open. Reflecting on the degree of alignment between your values, beliefs, and behavior becomes essential, particularly how your alignment is evidenced in times of high stress. Often under these conditions, we revert to patterns of behavior that are remnants of an immature self. Internal reflection can help us realize when we slip into these less than productive behavior patterns. As we share our vision and goals and admit when we have fallen short, we create a condition of interdependence and trust can be restored.

Be aware that once trust is broken, it is extremely difficult to rebuild. The very nature of trust itself has been undermined. An immediate apology and steps to remedy any harm done are essential. Then, vigilance to maintain and deepen trust will be in order, which means taking care to not repeat the offending behavior. Because trust is so tenuous and must be earned through your consistent actions and integrity, you generally only get one chance at rebuilding trust. Broken a second time, you will have earned the reputation of being untrustworthy.

Creating trust between you and among the members of your team is especially critical with teams composed of people with diverse backgrounds. Research has indicated that "members of culturally diverse teams express higher levels of mistrust than do their more homogeneous counterparts."[17] Yet, as we have recognized, culturally diverse teams function more creatively than do homogenous teams. They have "the potential to invent more options and create more solutions than single-culture teams." As Nancy Adler points out, "The productivity of the team does not depend on the presence or absence of diversity, but rather on how well diversity is managed."

If you have created or are a member of a diverse team whose members trust each other and you because of your competencies and integrity in addition to their personal relationship with you, you will observe a cohesiveness even when divergent opinions arise. Discussions will display a certain ease and effectiveness. The team's creativity will abound. They will help identify many alternative options and smart decisions. Members will increasingly demonstrate clear and realistic expectations of each other, an ease of engaging in projects together and an open and effective flow of information. They will relate to each other in a manner characterized by respect and safety, freely exchanging feedback and demonstrating positive attitudes with each other.

The point of "team," beyond doing the tasks at hand, is to:

· Expand the scope of available thinking and perspective of one individual

· Overcome blind spots

· Compensate for each other's limitations

· Provide an interactive environment for growth and expansion of each individual involved, who are learning about Living on Purpose and who are exploring their relationships with the outer world.

While your team of whatever size or diversity can successfully assist you in developing your dream, the team needs you primarily

---

[17] Adler, Nancy J. and Allison with Gundersen. 2008. *International Dimensions of Organizational Behavior.* 5th ed. Mason, Ohio: Cengage Thomas South-Western.

to be its *visionary leader, the CDO* (Chief Dream Officer). No one else can perform this function as no one else knows the origin or magical alchemy of your personal dream. Being true to yourself constitutes an essential dimension in the process of developing your dream and leading your team. Leading authentically—rooted in self-awareness—requires an alignment of your actions, values, and belief systems with who you are at your deepest core. Timothy E. Lagan describes authentic leadership as, "Being in tune with their own sense of self, knowing where they stand on important issues, and behaving accordingly." [18] This is the level of organizational leadership needed today in a world of confused values and motives. It goes beyond the management and leadership skills taught in university classrooms. Authentic leadership requires the integration of body, mind, emotion, *and spirit.* The spiritual element is reaching toward and incorporating into daily life that which is highest within us. Offer vision, support, and training, then let your team members do what they do best.

As you meet each challenge in your transition to bringing your Life on Purpose, you create, inspire, and lead a team of committed individuals pursuing the same. Now, you are a community of individuals breathing life into the business of work with volition and determination. You are no longer making a product or offering a service within the old-story confines of profit and loss. You are creating a relationship with the rest of the world, evoking the greatness that has always resided within you. This is the *real* business of a Life on Purpose, changing the world with the support of a team of committed people.

---

[18] Lagan, Ph.D., Timothy E., Examining authentic leadership: Development of a four-dimensional scale and identification of anomological network, (2007), State University of New York at Albany.

Intent into Action
Tools for Chapter 5: Committed People: Your Team

The next most important concept to affix in your mind is that YOU DON'T HAVE TO DO IT ALONE. If your dream's statement and vision are clear in your mind and exciting to your heart, others will be compelled to support your efforts, even if that is simply to mentor you in preparing for a new job or career. In addition to helping do the work, the right team members can offer diverse perspectives and insight, provide ideas for brainstorming, and fill in where your own expertise might be limited. Keep in mind that team members need not be full time on your payroll; many can be engaged by the hour or job. The journey from chaos into a new story need not be a solitary one.

Every person who ends up on your team regardless of the role they may play, adds his or her contribution to the collective strengths of the team. If you wisely seek individuals who have strengths that compensate for the limitations of others, you will create a stronger and more effective team. This applies to: what individuals know, skills and experience they have, and financial or physical resources they might be willing to add to the project. Damaging tendencies—poor thinking habits, limiting beliefs, low self-image, constant complaining—are ones you won't be able to change in others; therefore be cautious of engaging people with an abundance of these. They can potentially undermine your hard work, both personally and professionally. Seek experienced people with good self-image, and who identify with your dream for a big head start.

Understanding some basics of communication and personality profiles will help you match individuals with the most suitable roles for them to play. It will also boost your effectiveness in communicating with them. Seek the systems that are simple to learn while offering invaluable and usable insight.

Remember that there are individuals who would be willing to consider creative plans for compensation, and remember that the cheapest is not always the best choice. The quality of your product or services' branding must match the quality of your dream.

The process for assembling a team of committed people includes going beyond the standard application and interview techniques. Getting a sense of their personal dreams, their communication and personality styles, and their personal strengths will give you extremely valuable information for making wise hiring decisions.

- *Don't try to do it all yourself.*

- *Look for specific strengths and limit those with the damaging tendencies.*

- *Learn the basics of one or two communication and personality profile systems.*

- *Be creative in your compensation offers.*

6
Strategies for Aligned Action

There is a vitality, a life-force, an energy, a quickening that is translated through you into action and because there is only one of you in all of time, this expression is unique. And if you block it, it will never exist through any other medium and be lost.

—MARTHA GRAHAM (1894–1991)

We discussed in an earlier chapter that if you climb the staircase inside a skyscraper one step at a time, eventually stepping onto the top of the building will be the next step. By the same token, standing at the bottom of the stairwell looking up will not get you to the top. Wishing you were at the top will not get you there. Even believing you can get to the top will not get you to the top of the building. Looking, wishing, and believing without action is fantasy. You have to lift your foot, place it on the first step, and raise your body to the level of that step, then lift your other foot, place it on the next step, and raise your body to the level of the second step, and repeat over and over again. Finally, after many, many action steps, the very last step will put you in contact with your goal.

Until action is taken, nothing in the outer world will change and our dreams will remain a fantasy.

The hardest step on this ladder of self-discovery is putting the knowledge of our identity to work in the physical world by taking action in alignment with that identity.

In order for us to make our interaction with the outer world, at some point there must be action. In order for us to Live on Purpose, that action must align with our true identity.

Cellular Wisdom at Work

During development of the fetus, the maturation of neuronal pathways is dependent upon activity within the immature circuits. Without this activity, pathways fail to develop. Complex circuits do not form.

For example, the visual system of animals reared in darkness remains in an immature state later in life. Unable to see clearly, these animals fail to discriminate visual objects. Stimulation of immature pathways determines the full development of mature complex circuits required for full function.

Taking the steps that promote the development of our dream constitutes as essential an element as does activity within the developing nervous system.

Message to the Reader

While the preparation you've already made has been significant in shaping the future of your career, professional, or business vision, the activity you now engage in is essential to its development. The actions you take now are not simply implementing the plan that you developed. They will mature those plans and shape them in a way that makes them functional. It is in the interactions between your actions and the external world that you will learn much about what really works for you, what does not work for you, and will begin to refine the ultimate expression of your professional life.

Your dream, your idea for expressing your identity and Purpose into the outer world, should remain fairly stable except for expanding as your perspective grows, until it is time to let this one go and begin a new dream. Your vision, the picture you hold in your mind of you doing or living your dream, is more fluid in that the picture might shift when you find out what works and what doesn't work for you when you start taking action steps. You will recall how Maria's vision for her open house changed when confronted with the reality of her small budget. Her dream, to make and sell designer jewelry did not change at all. Action can also reveal flaws in your plan, invisible on paper. Action can thus help you reshape the more malleable aspects of pursuing your Purpose, thus maturing your vision and plan, adding new clarity and refinement to them.

How you choose to go about taking these actions can mean the difference between repeating history and writing a new story. Alignment provides the key.

> *Aligned action is taking the next step toward your dream. It is the combination of action plus your alignment of thoughts, emotions, beliefs, words, and values with your inner self.*

It is taking the next step on the stairway inside the skyscraper toward the top of the building *in alignment* with your larger self.

When you say you want to be an honest person, but you believe you have to tell a lie in order for someone to do what you want them to or to think well of you, you are not in alignment with the personal value of honesty. When you think you are stuck with nowhere to go, say that you don't know why opportunities don't come to you, and deny the existence of your personal power, you are not in alignment with your inner nature. When your thoughts align with your beliefs, align with your words and your inner being, but you act in a way that denies that alignment, you are *not* taking aligned action. Doubting yourself is

> *In order for there to be aligned action, your thoughts, emotions, beliefs, words, values, and actions must be in agreement, congruent, with the truth of your identity—your oneness with life.*

not being in alignment. Believing you are less than magnificent is not being aligned. Operating from fear is not aligning with your true identity.

You might say, "But, Joan, no one I know has all of those things lined up in agreement. How can I possibly get there?" It's highly likely that you don't know anyone who lives their life in full alignment. That's not surprising. That *is* the old story. It's why the old systems can't carry us into a new and better future. It is why, determining the direction of the new story, begins with you. As to how you can get there, that's the reason for this book and the others in the Cellular Wisdom series.

We have become so accustomed to moving through our lives without the slightest recognition or acknowledgement of our greatness, that we have come to believe it doesn't really exist.

We have been trying to function with a tremendous handicap.

Beliefs can be changed, such as: working hard, sacrificing, and effacing one's self will not carry us into a brighter future. Values can also be changed. Words, thoughts, emotions, beliefs, and values can *all* be changed to serve you better. We can continue to bring forth more of **our true identity**. The closer all the other elements get to agreement with the larger self, the more powerful they, and you, become.

We are *not* saying that hard work is wrong or unnecessary. We are not saying that you will not have to work to achieve your dream. We are saying that holding a value of hard work of and by itself is an old story. Be willing to invest however much effort it takes in order to realize your dream. It will often entail hard work that might last for days, weeks, months, or even years. Understand that when hard work is held as a *value*, ennobled if you will, it becomes an end in itself, and a self-fulfilling prophecy requiring endless hard work. Go beyond that thinking into a realm where a Life on Purpose is a primary value that holds the option open for serendipity, synchronicity, and miracles. A *value* of hard work precludes the possibility of serendipity and miracles. This is an example of how our values shape our lives in subtle ways and why it behooves us to become more aware and mindful of what values will serve us best moving forward.

Taking action is a given in the development of a dream, but the difference between old story actions and aligned actions is the difference between continuing on the same old course and writing a new story. As Albert Einstein has suggested:

"It is insane to continue taking the same action while expecting a different outcome."

Old story action has many signals that let us know when we are repeating old patterns. The following are a few of them:

- Circumventing the plan to take the course that is easiest, the most comfortable, or what we think others expect of us will move us off course of Living on Purpose.

- Meeting many frustrations or feeling tired or defeated or stuck are signals of acting from the old story.

- Any time we find ourselves forcing the issue in order to receive the desired benefit, any time we know that something is "not right," any time our prospects feel like they are contracting, we are not taking aligned action.

- Impatience out of control and beyond reason is evidence of the failure of the old story to give us peace or meaning.

Even success, if forcefully achieved by old story methods and values, generally leaves us feeling hollow and unfulfilled because it isn't the money or prestige that we really want. What we truly want is a connection with our inner identity, a relationship with our deepest inner self inside us all, and this cannot be attained by the old methods.

Aligned action feels good, feels exciting and expanding, and gives the fire of passion hand-in-hand with inner peace in the knowledge of who you are.

- Aligned action *feels* like the next step.
- It is easy and not forced, although it may stretch us.
- Everything flows smoothly into place at its optimal time.
- The plan will likely be altered or circumvented on occasion, but will result in speeding us toward the dream.
- Aligned action will leave you alert to new opportunities.

Take the example of climbing the stairs to get to the top of the skyscraper. You can get to the top by sheer will power, determination, and hard work, taking one step after another until you get there. This is one type of success and one we are all familiar with. But suppose, in alignment with your inner resources, you listen to the voice that suggests you look up from your feet, and you see a sign telling you that out this door is an escalator. You now might deviate from the written plan and be *carried* up however many flights of stairs the escalator services. At the top of the escalator you might find a bank of elevators that can carry you up even farther, maybe all the way to the top. Your dream did not change. But your vision and plan of *how* you would get there was altered to allow the serendipitous awareness of an escalator to register as an opportunity worth pursuing. This is the potential reward of aligned action and Living on Purpose and suggests a new and different kind of success.

The following are some guidelines for developing alignment, before one can take aligned action.

1) Know what alignment means

Alignment starts with your relationship with yourself, spreads to those with whom you interact, and eventually by the ripple effect to the world at large.

Your relationship with yourself is first and foremost the knowledge of who you truly are.

It is your possession of qualities of the inner resources that lie within your own life force. Your relationship with others is first and foremost the knowledge of your own *and the others'* heritage. This knowledge demands that you treat yourself and others with respect and care worthy of our expansive nature.

Alignment means:

- having a grasp of your inner limitless resources—however you can grasp it

- believing that you are capable and worthy because of your heritage

- thinking "Yes, I can do this"

- feeling confident of your identity and ability and excited about the prospects for your future

- saying that you are willing and able to do the task at hand

- knowing that this alignment can lead to unprecedented opportunity

- acting with the courage of your conviction

When you can relate to yourself and everyone you encounter from a position of shared origin and alignment with it, your world will change.

2) Know yourself; connect with your larger self

Start with what you do know, your strength development plan, and concentrate on your personal strengths. Continue to discover other positive aspects of your true nature. Look for evidence of the inner, expansive resources in the lives of people around you and in the lives of individuals you might read or hear about.

Every story you encounter about someone beating odds that seemed insurmountable will help you see the inevitability of your own human potential.

Once you recognize it readily in others, you will be ready to recognize these qualities in yourself. Ask a friend who is insightful to help you identify them in you. Allow yourself to accept this part of who you are; mentally and emotionally "own" the quality; let the knowledge seep into your conscious awareness.

- I *did* do that, didn't I?

- It *did* take courage to take that step, didn't it?

- I *did* feel connected to something bigger than myself at that moment.

- When I get quiet inside, I *can* feel a kinship with creation.

Cellular Wisdom at Work

 The influence of environment on the functioning of cells, tissues, organs, and animals has been documented extensively. The supply of nutrients, the quality of nutrients, and the number of cells, tissues, organs or animals in a specific area, all influence the operation of these biological entities. There is a balance of elements that yields an optimal environment for the growth and development of cells, tissues, organs, and animals.

The optimal environment for the growth and development of a dream likewise requires a steady supply of quality nutrients. The optimal environment will be rich in the elements that foster growth and development of the individuals involved: optimism, positive expectations, values, freeing beliefs, hope, encouraging words and appreciation of self and others, and recognition of and alignment with the elements of a larger, grander, creative life with a new story.

3) Provide an optimal environment for success

If we observe our environment and activities as making up the nutrients offered our different natures—physical, mental, emotional, and spiritual—we can see how we would want to provide the best available to us. For example, a constant influx of worry, anger, and despair would give little nutritive value to our emotional nature. And an environment of judgment and recrimination does little to feed a healthy spiritual nature.

- Nourish your mind with books, newsletters, tapes, classes, lectures, and conversations which introduce you to new ideas, concepts, and knowledge

- Nourish your emotional life with acts and thoughts of acceptance, support, safety, encouragement, laughter, and celebration

- Nourish your spiritual life with appreciation, self-discovery, growth, and expansion of awareness and vision

Providing a rich environment for these aspects of your life will also provide an atmosphere for nurturing your growth and development as an human living a new story. Surround yourself with people, situations, and opportunities to support and enrich the atmosphere of alignment. This is the optimal environment for taking action toward your dreams, for giving yourself the best possible opportunity for success. Changing your environment won't happen overnight, but if you are committed, practice new habits that would serve you more effectively, and consistently seek to improve your personal environment, you *will* get there.

4) Consciously focus your mental activities and thoughts.

If we focus on a successful business or dream, it will follow. If we focus on lack of money or opportunity, *that* will follow, even though more lack is not what we really wanted.

We will experience more of whatever we focus our attention upon.

Most of us have stumbled through our lives not fully knowing or understanding this with, not surprisingly, mixed results. In the moments we got enthused about something we wanted to do, we tended to focus on that desirable end result and create desirable results. In moments of worry or frustration or concern, we tended to focus on the outcomes we did not want. We frequently got the unwanted outcome anyway, as a result of our focus and the unknowing application of creation.

If lack of knowledge has gotten us where we are now, just think of where we might be able to go with the knowledge and conscious use of our mental focus!

This doesn't work as simply as wishful thinking; we don't automatically get whatever we wish for. We don't get whatever we think about just by thinking it.

Without conscious awareness, our thoughts tend to scatter all over the place instead of being focused and aligned. Everyone has an energetic pattern they have developed over the course of their lives.

Some, developed patterns in a foundation of worry. Others developed patterns of comfort or money or struggle-to-make-ends-meet. *Not* everyone knows how to focus a connection with the mental energy of their goal and their true, inner self.

Intended focus on an idea allows that idea to gather creative energy and grow. Everything created by someone was first an idea in his or her mind.

If your actions and goal are in the direction of a new, easier job, but your thoughts are ambivalent, what do you think your life patterns will result in? Getting the job, or not? If your words are negative, your beliefs are that you don't deserve the new position, what is likely the result? If your emotions are fearful of the state of the economy and its impact on jobs, and you value hard work what is the likely result?

You can see how it is more complicated than just thinking something and it happening. Deliberately align your focus, your thoughts, words, emotions, beliefs, values, and actions so that they all agree with each other and with your deepest inner self. Once this is accomplished with consistency, and it will take diligent effort, you will have access to a new and extremely powerful tool for pursuing your dreams and your Life on Purpose.

Positive expectations (emotion) have merit and power. But by themselves they can be circumvented by essentially different thoughts, words, values, and beliefs. Words can have merit and power. But if no other elements align with them, their power is short-circuited. **Alignment is the key**! When something in the chain is out of alignment, you will experience resistance. This resistance might come in the form of a feeling of something not being quite right or in the form of frustration or in the form of the task taking three times as long as it should or in the form of a piece of equipment breaking down. Generally, without resistance everything runs smoothly and easily. However, sometimes things beyond our control, external circumstances, must come into alignment before results are realized. Not all failure to flow is due to resistance. You can readily determine whether you are out of alignment somewhere by the presence of resistance. Monitor your internal responses as they are your guide to your true path. Whenever they signal a resistance, stop and revisit your alignment until you experience the flow of liberation.

If you get out of alignment, and you will, there are tools that can be extremely useful in getting back on track. The first is called "reframing."

Randy Pausch's Story

Randy Pausch was a Carnegie-Mellon Professor who gave his "Last Lecture" and wrote a book by the same title. Dying of multiple tumors in his liver, aware that he was leaving his wife and three young children behind, Randy epitomized the power of this strategy. Jeffrey Zaslow, the co-author of Randy's book, asks him in an interview, "So your book begins with the line, 'I have an engineering problem.' Why did you start it that way?" Randy's answer represents one of the best reframing examples I have heard. He answered, "Facing your own death is something that you can look at in a myriad of ways. Looking at it as an engineering problem for me frames it as—I have things I can do that will make a difference—things that will help my wife, things that will help my kids. The more existential side of this, *the navel gazing, oh, woe is me*, that's not going to help anybody. So for me to frame it as an engineering problem puts the focus: OK, I may not like the situation but what can I do with the remaining time to make the best outcome I can for everybody that I love."

Charting the development of your career or business pales in comparison to preparing for death, yet the power of Randy's reframing strategy moves us when we listen to Randy's words. He could have chosen to spend the final days of his life feeling depressed and in despair. But Randy chose to reframe his condition from "fatal disease" to "engineering problem," and spent the precious time he had left lecturing about living life to the fullest in every moment he was granted to be here. Randy was able to keep himself out of the crippling negative emotions that by all rights his condition warranted. He has provided the world with a powerful and memorable example of reframing as well as the congruence of alignment. He was aligned in thought, word, actions, beliefs, and values—*with his condition* and his true identity.

Appreciation

The other incredibly valuable tool to getting aligned is appreciation. When you take the time to notice and appreciate all the ease, beauty, courage, intelligence, grace, integration, love, and wisdom that permeates your world, you touch the new story within you. This activity *overlooks* the imperfections, the misaligned conditions, the lack of awareness that also abound. It allows you to circumvent what you don't like in your world and connect with that which resonates deepest inside, much like seeing your goal or vision on the other side of a pine board. Anytime you feel resistance creeping into your experience, stop that very moment and find at least twenty-five things to appreciate about yourself and everything and everyone around you. If a list of twenty-five doesn't do the trick, go to fifty or one hundred. Eventually you will feel your alignment shift. That is when you know you have done enough for now.

Appreciating small successes opens the door for continued growth and expansion in a manner that aligns with your vision for your career, profession, or business. Nothing is too small or too large to be appreciated in your work environment, from the fact that today you have a job to realizing your biggest dream, from a piece of equipment that always operates dependably to christening your new building, from the cooperative efforts of a single helper, to the integration of an entire organization. Small successes give confidence that can lead to greater success. The more you appreciate, the more you will have in your life to appreciate.

Several years ago, *Fast Company*, a magazine that "empowers innovators to challenge convention and create the future of business," interviewed a project manager on how he regularly brought in his projects before or on time. Sought after by many companies, *Fast Company* interviewed the manager about the secret to his success. His response was, "My team and I spend eighty percent of our time thinking and twenty percent of our time doing." He continued, saying that they made fewer mistakes because they thought through processes thoroughly, exploring many potential scenarios and identifying their responses to those scenarios.

I would like to take this great insight a step further and suggest that if we spend eighty percent of our time and energy planning, envisioning, reviewing, *and aligning* our resources and focus with our true selves and twenty percent of our time and energy taking action, we would find that each action is more concise, on target, and effective. Now that we have at least a rough idea of alignment and aligned action, it is time to begin taking those first steps. The following are important to keep in mind:

- Pay attention to your priorities. Act on your first priorities each day. You will find that you get the most important things done.

- The next step will feel natural and easy, although it may require some stretching. Remember, you can't get from the sidewalk to the top of the skyscraper in one giant step.

- Attend to the various aspects of timing.
  - Green beans are not ready to pick the day after planting them.
  - Are you ahead of the wave or has it already passed you by?
  - Are you overstaying in a situation? If you lack energy, passion, and enthusiasm; if you are feeling under-appreciated, under-valued, and under-paid; if you are not utilizing a wide range of your talents, skills, interests, and abilities; if there are no opportunities for growth or expansion; or if you accomplished what you signed up to do long ago and need to get on with the next project, you may be overstaying.

- Stay alert to new opportunities. They may not present themselves conspicuously. Develop a radar-like sensitivity to them. Sometimes an offer that doesn't look like much at first glance can lead to an unexpected brilliant new possibility.

- Pay attention to your intuition.

- Be accountable. Answer to someone—your team members, mentor, advisors, or coach—for your progress. This can help you to stay on track, to continue taking action steps, and to focus your alignment through the habit of making a regularly scheduled report.

Cellular Wisdom at Work

 Researchers studying the developing brain observe that as neurons migrate from their place of origin to their place of destination they project an ending tentatively in one direction. Watching them in real time you can see them either continue in that direction, withdraw from going in that direction, make a ninety-degree turn, or sometimes a turn in a completely different direction. No two neurons do this exactly the same.

Watching the movie of neurons moving in the developing brain gives you a sense of the majesty of the process of finding their way. Not all directions were productive. They simply withdrew from those that were not and continue to pursue other directions some of which were productive. These actions flowed as effortlessly as the movements that characterize a well rehearsed dance. Such is the process of self-discovery and growing a dream.

Obstacles will arise in our activities. No one can maintain perfect alignment all the time, and no one is surrounded by only individuals who can maintain perfect alignment. Because we are imperfect humans living in an imperfect world, we will create and encounter obstacles: snags with labor, supplies, communication, and colleagues, failure of steps or systems, rejection of ideas. How we react to them will determine our ultimate success or failure. Navigating around or through obstacles or challenges is far more productive than becoming stuck or stopped.

"As a leader," remarks Faye E. Coleman, president & CEO of Westover Consultants, and chair of the board of Leadership Washington, "no matter the community or project in which you are involved,

having a clear vision and keeping it in focus will provide a necessary compass to navigate the turbulent waters of today's ever-changing business environment."

Allow the dream itself—the ultimate goal—to serve as the criteria for evaluation and the vision to serve as the compass direction (West) for navigation. Are you moving toward your dream and vision or away from them?

Rejection—of your idea, your proposal, your application, your inquiry—is one of the most common obstacles encountered. Not everyone will see its merits. Not everyone will love your new book. Not everyone will accept your proposal. Not everyone will want to hire you. Often when we bump up against rejection we feel that our humanity, our existence, we ourselves, are what is being rejected. The tendency is to take the rejection personally, therefore, as criticism of our shortcomings or of our dream, and to give up on it. Rejection and failure are two of the most pervasive obstacles we will face, all too often resulting in giving up on our dreams.

Persistence is required if we are to pursue our dreams. There are numerous examples of individuals hitting brick walls and continuing in spite of it. More than 200 investors rejected the proposal of Howard Schultz to expand Starbucks beyond the five stores in Seattle. He persisted. Today, Starbucks is the leading retailer, roaster, and brand of specialty coffee in the world, with over 17,000 stores in forty-nine countries. What allowed Howard Schultz to persist in spite of the negative response to his repeated proposals? Schultz believed strongly in the validity of his dream. He saw the vision of his little coffee shops springing up in many cities. He thought about how it would all come about. He talked with his business executives about his vision. He valued his idea to expand. His mental focus aligned with succeeding in spite of repeated rejection. This fueled the persistence that carried him through the obstacles to unprecedented success.

In his book, *The Road to Success is Paved with Failure: How Hundreds of Famous People Triumphed Over Inauspicious Beginnings, Crushing Rejection, Humiliating Defeats and Other Speed Bumps Along Life's Highway* (Little, Brown and Company, 2001), Joey Green recounts multiple stories of failure and success.

- Marilyn Monroe, a Hollywood sex goddess, was dropped in 1947 by Twentieth Century-Fox after one year under contract because Production Chief Darryl Zanuck thought she was unattractive.

- John F. Kennedy ran for president of his freshman college class at Harvard University and lost.

- Dr. Seuss's first book, *And to Think That I Saw It on Mulberry Street,* was rejected by twenty-seven publishing houses, and Seuss considered burning the manuscript. He went on to write more than forty best-selling children's books.

- Michael Jordan was cut from his high school's varsity football team.

- Sigmund Freud's first book, *The Interpretation of Dreams,* netted the author $250 in royalties in the first eight years after its publication.

- Elvis Presley was told by his high school teacher that he could not sing.

- Barbra Walters was told to stay out of television.

- John Grisham's first novel, *A Time to Kill,* was rejected by sixteen agents and a dozen publishing houses.

- Walt Disney's first cartoon production company went bankrupt.

If Marilyn Monroe, John F. Kennedy, Dr. Seuss, Michael Jordan, Sigmund Freud, Elvis Presley, Barbra Walters, John Grisham, or Walt Disney had turned away from pursuing their dreams because of perceived failure or rejection, they would not have attained the considerable success that characterizes their contributions, and the world would be a poorer place because of it.

As you begin to take action unfolding your dream, making your business, career, or profession real in the world, you will sooner or later encounter what Randy Pausch calls "a brick wall." Fear of failure often immobilizes us. Successful professionals, business and career people tell us if you haven't failed, you haven't done enough. Randy believes that we encounter the brick wall to find out how much we really want something. In his book, *The Last Lecture* (Hyperion, 2008), he admits that he was not allowed entrance into Carnegie Mellon when he first applied. But because he wanted to go there so badly, he engaged allies to help him and he was ultimately admitted. What a different place Carnegie Mellon would be today without the contributions of the famed Randy Pausch.

Failure can make us aware of the need for change or have the effect of stopping us from recognizing opportunities that might not have emerged had we stayed on our previous path. Successful people make great use of what they learn from mistakes and consider failure as a part of that growth process. Successful people on a path of Purpose add alignment to that equation and do not lose sight of who they truly are and what their dream is. We are not perfectly aligned all the time, our actions will inevitably result in the failure of steps, processes, systems, even projects, but NOT of the dream itself. The dream will endure as long as we don't abandon it. Reframing what the challenge is, using the vision as the focal point, appreciating our options and successes, refining the vision or the plan, and changing words, thoughts, emotions, and limiting beliefs to align with our core identity are all effective tools to navigate through obstacles like failure and rejection.

Facing adversity has great value, for as we meet the challenge, we utilize talents and abilities previously unknown. Napoleon Hill, author of *Think and Grow Rich* (Tribeca Books, 2011), one of the best-selling books of all time and presidential advisor to Franklin D. Roosevelt from 1933–36, articulated this point of aligned wisdom:

You have chosen to develop your dream. I honor you for your choice. You are among the minority of individuals who choose to actualize their dreams. Know that what you can conceive and believe you can achieve, regardless of current fiscal conditions in the world and changing job and corporate cultures. If you *reframe* rejection, failure, and problems to "opportunities for learning and growth," you will have transitioned into the resonance of eagerness, transformation, and success.

> *"What the mind of man can conceive and believe, it can achieve."*

Remember the lesson from board breaking from Chapter 2? If you keep your focus on your vision—the activity of living your dream—you will not be stopped by obstacles. With boards, going right through them is how you navigate to your goal. Sometimes the most effective navigation will be to go around the obstacle, or over it, or under it, or to slip in sideways. No matter how you decided to navigate an obstacle, your dream and vision will always get you back to West.

> *When you keep your focus firmly planted on the vision you hold of your dream, that is where you will end up regardless of what arises in your path.*

If you add *alignment* to your activities, alignment of your words, thoughts, beliefs, values, and actions with your vision and your identity, the obstacles in your way dissolve.

Cellular Wisdom at Work

Homeostasis, the regulation of the body's internal environment to maintain a stable, constant condition, represents a fundamental principle of how the body is structured and functions. The ability to sustain this dynamic equilibrium through adjustment and regulation was recognized by Claude Bernard, a French physiologist, in 1865. Many different mechanisms contribute to this capability, including the autonomic nervous system. Two components of the autonomic nervous system, the sympathetic system, which arouses to action, and the parasympathetic system, which restores balance, work in concert to maintain homeostasis in many internal organs in the body, including the heart.

We can override the normal balancing mechanisms of the autonomic nervous system by perceiving situations as threatening and sustaining our arousal. This sustained activity of the sympathetic nervous system results in sustained arousal, stress, and frequently lead to cardiovascular disease and other health imbalances.

Reframing the situation as less threatening allows us to balance the heightened arousal and reduce the cardiovascular activity. Positive emotions allow us to see the possibilities and opportunities even amidst stressful situations such as that of perceived failure and return the body to a state of homeostasis.

The constant pressure of keeping pace in a speeding world provides the perfect storm of circumstances for keeping the sympathetic nervous system on alert, ever ready for fight or flight. So does the constant barrage of obstacles demanding our attention and solution. We feel we must hurry to keep up; we feel we must defend our positions; we feel we must push ourselves to produce more, faster; we feel if we let down our guard for even a moment, we will lose out completely. Lose what? Our jobs, our prospects, our positions in the world, our means of survival, ourselves. In this context, failure equates emotionally with loss of survival and takes on enormous connotations, and as a result we seek success at all costs. If we don't learn to manage the stresses of modern living, we will find our taking action to be a frantic race for survival itself, with our health, relationships, and peace of mind crumbling around us. Let's see if we can't put this into a context that supports us.

Message to the Reader

It isn't failure that leads to success, even though it is a frequently experienced component. It is our resilience in *response* to failure that leads to success.

Pulitzer prize winner Paul Salopek comments to Peter Han, "If you fear not, if you're too comfortable, if you've made yourself invulnerable, you've built sort of, you know, a profitable blockade or palisade around you, I think you are going to miss out on some of these possibilities that flow by, that other people may attribute to serendipity, but may or may not be serendipitous. If you miss that, then I think that just constricts your horizons one notch further." What Salopek is suggesting is that putting yourself out there, taking risks of failure and not building walls of safety around you, is the sequence that can lead to unexpected opportunities.

> *If we aren't open to the possibility of failure we will not see the opportunities for success.*

Highly resilient people have been shown to cultivate positive emotions through the use of humor, relaxation techniques, and optimistic thinking as reported by psychologists Michele M. Tugade and Barbara L. Fredrickson in their article, "Resilient Individuals Use Positive Emotions to Bounce Back From Negative Emotional Experiences." Positive emotions prove beneficial in reducing stress, promoting positive coping strategies, and "infusing ordinary events with positive meaning."

The reason that positive emotions have such impact is explained by Barbara L. Fredrickson's "Broaden-and-Build" theory of positive emotions. Negative emotions restrict our thoughts and actions in the moment as we revert to instinctual patterns of behavior, for example, to attack when angry, to flee when afraid.

Those experiencing positive emotions in the midst of stress reduce the cardiovascular arousal initiated by stress.

The wisdom of our bodies suggests that the key to resilience is managing stress through the conscious manipulation of our emotions. Positive emotions calm the fight or flight responses of the sympathetic nervous system. Shifting from emotions related to stress (frustration, anxiety, worry, anger) to positive emotions (calmness, confidence, optimism, joy) takes some effort to accomplish, but is essential for moving into a Life on Purpose and a better story. We've already discussed the merits of reframing events or circumstances and of appreciation. These strategies are about getting one's self aligned. Let's examine some of the strategies that can help manage the emotional stress you will encounter.

1) Rely on your plan. You have already thought of many of the steps needed to arrive at your goal. There are times when deviating from the plan as circumstances present themselves is necessary, just as there are times when navigating around, under, or through circumstances may be what is needed. But just because you had to navigate through a situation doesn't mean that you then abandon the plan. It is your road map. Keep coming back to the plan, refining it as you gain experience and insight. Knowing that you already have a map in place will dispel the stress of not knowing what comes next.

2) Let go of an idea that is creating stress, such as the need for your dream to take a predetermined physical form or the need for perfection. We often become so invested in the physical details of our vision, that we might not even recognize it happening if it shows up in a different form. Vision is meant to give you the sense of direction (West) toward which the subconscious mind gathers creative energy.

Early in my life, I decided that I would derive the greatest meaning from life by living a life dedicated to others. I entered the convent at seventeen years of age, determined to be the perfect Dominican Sister. In the eleven years I remained in the convent, this strategy resulted in my choosing to follow rules and regulations to a point that I eventually felt so restricted that I was going to dry up and die inside. My strategy to reach for perfection proved unsuccessful.

It was not long after obtaining my Ph.D. and becoming a faculty member that I began once again to implement my perfection strategy. I was going to be the perfect faculty member, researcher, teacher, laboratory director, course supervisor, then Chair of a department and Director of a research center. Once again, my strategy to reach for perfection resulted in my feeling crushed by these demands.

Leaving academia and founding Beyond Success, LLC, I resolved to relinquish my unsuccessful strategy of seeking perfection. I searched for other strategies in classes, with new friends and esteemed mentors. This exploration allowed me to discover a most empowering strategy. No longer was the emphasis on me, but rather, shifted to the value I could offer people in helping them evoke their greatness. This strategy has proved enormously effective for me as I have reframed how I find meaning in my life. It allows me to bring my experience from multiple domains to the service of others in a pursuit that touches the essence of life.

3) Get details onto paper or computer file rather than trying to carry so much data around in your head. Cognitive neuroscientists have told us for some time that the brain can process only about seven things simultaneously. If we attempt to hold and process more than seven information items, we are likely to create a situation that is inherently stressful. There is great value in remembering information externally, whether you use a mind map, entries into Outlook, a project management program, a project list combined with a daily to do list, or any other organizational system. Once the information is recorded externally, your brain is then freed up to process more critical data and stress is reduced.

David Allen, the creator of Getting Things Done organizational systems and education, speaks of "the stress of opportunity." As you begin taking the actions required to create or reengineer your work environment, you will be bombarded by opportunities, tasks, and challenges. Managing the stress requires you to manage the information, specifically, meaningful information, which will increase with every action that you take.

As I began Beyond Success, the many different projects that needed to be begun clamored for my attention. As I began initial steps on each of these components, it became clear that I needed a mechanism to track my progress. I wanted a way to see all projects and my next-step actions. About that time I learned about mind mapping and a software program called Mind Manager. The program assists me in creating a mind map that allows me to see all of my projects and the next action steps on one sheet of paper.

Keeping your eye on the mission and the passion that fuels your career, profession, or business will help you to continually monitor your progress in the use of systems which allow you, in David Allen's words to "surf on top of" information rather than being "buried" by it.

4) Manage your energy and your time will be managed as a result. Your energy is as valuable as your money, and if you don't use your energy effectively, you will be setting yourself up for increased stress levels and potential failure of your dream. Planning how you use your energy is time well spent. Aligning your resources, thoughts, words, emotions, beliefs, and actions with your true inner self is absolutely essential for moving forward with minimal stress toward your Life on Purpose. Here are some helpful ideas:

- What are the tasks that sustain your energy? Completing these will help ensure that you keep heading in the right direction. The tendency is to over-estimate what you can accomplish in a day and under-estimate what you can accomplish in a year.

- Keep your energy in focus so that you will consistently be able to successfully accomplish the most important items on the daily list, even if it is only two items. It is an important signal to your subconscious mind that you are having daily small successes. Every small success in the direction of your goal takes you closer. Target one hundred percent completion with eighty percent effort. This allows for some distractions, but not significant ones. Congratulate yourself for completing more tasks than were on the list.

- Guard diligently against energy-wasters. If you aren't careful, you can deplete your energy, spending entire days (which then turn into weeks and months) reading and answering emails and text messages, nosing around on the Internet, conversing with friends or family, or reading the newspaper, to name the most common culprits. If you make it a habit to explore your energy expenditures before engaging in any of these distracting activities, you will not find yourself lacking in energy. You will accomplish what you set out to accomplish and will not have to deal with the stress that results from wasting your energy and not accomplishing your goals.

- Twenty percent of your prospective customers will bring eighty percent of your income; spend eighty percent of your energy developing the most promising twenty percent. Don't waste your energy on the unproductive eighty percent.

Cellular Wisdom at Work

 Risk is built into the very fabric of our body's cells, tissues, organs, and systems. Examples abound. Neurons that control reproduction, which reside close to the pituitary in the adult, are born in the nose of the fetus, a long way from their destination. They must migrate and find their way during development to their destination in the hypothalamus, just above the pituitary. The risk, the chance of losing their way, is great. Traveling together they find their way. Neurons which leave the cluster die.

Neurons, unlike other cells, store no nutrients, in spite of their vital function. Why would they take such an enormous risk? Freed from the need to use resources to amass nutrients and convert them into storable forms, neurons devote all of their energies to observing and evaluating ongoing conditions. This resultant sensitivity allows neurons to detect any minute change in the internal environment quickly, and gives them the significant advantage of appropriate and quick response times, even though it puts them at mortal risk.

Staying alert to changes in our interior environments, particularly in the midst of uncertainty, allows us to detect whether the actions we begin to take truly reflect the unfolding of our authentic path or instead constitute deviations from that path. Like our neurons, at this early stage in the development or re-engineering of our work, our energies must focus on assessing our environments and responding in such a fashion as to stay true to our authentic path. To do this, we have to risk the validity of our vision and our plan. Risk is inherent in achieving success.

Author's Story

Before I knew it, it was time for me to act on my dream, even though I had not proven to myself I could actually do it. Taking specific actions to make my business real constituted a great risk for me, but one I had to take. If I could not take this risk, I could not offer my services to help others evoke their greatness. This was scary for me.

I think I've always understood that one cannot accomplish something significant without taking risks. The question was which risks were the smart risks to take? As I thought about it more and more I realized it was a smart risk for me to start a small business, considering my success in running a laboratory for many years, which is essentially like running a small business. This, together with the preparations I had made to gain fiscal freedom so that I could devote time to developing the business and reach out to the many connections I had made in the Boston area over the past eighteen years, contributed to my assessment of this as a smart risk. The challenge was I had to know that I could do what I asked my clients to do: take risks and evoke my greatness. If I was unable to do this, I could not legitimately offer my services to others. I took the risk and have never looked back since.

Bill Strickland's Story, Part II

Remember Bill Strickland? We met him speaking at Harvard Business School in an earlier chapter about the Manchester Craftsmen's Guild, a tiny neighborhood arts center that he founded and which became Manchester Bidwell. Strickland describes how Manchester Bidwell came about. "It happened because the clueless nineteen year old trusted his unspoken intuition that the human spirit is remarkably resilient, and that even in damaged and disadvantaged lives, and in circumstances where the odds seem hopelessly stacked against you, there is endless potential waiting to be freed." Bill Strickland refused to be limited by "the cautious little voice."

Bill grew up in poverty in a ghetto in Pittsburgh. One morning during his senior year Bill was "ambling unhappily" in the hall of his high school going to homeroom when he caught the smell of fresh coffee. Following the aroma, he entered the art room to find a white guy with his head bowed forward rocking gently on his stool, leaning over a turntable. He was shaping clay. As Bill watched, the ball of clay seemed to come magically alive. The man, Frank Ross, was his art teacher from his sophomore year, who had taken a sabbatical during Bill's junior year. "You want to try it?" Frank asked Bill. Soon Frank was instructing Bill about how to hold his elbows and use his hands and his body to shape the clay. In Frank's classroom, Bill experienced something very different, which he describes as "an atmosphere of purpose, calmness, and sanity," completely foreign to the streets of the ghetto. As he worked more with the clay Bill began to believe that something extraordinary was within his grasp. Bill was escaping his "poverty of spirit." This awakening did not, however, extend to Bill's other classes. Learning of his falling grades, Frank Ross spoke up for Bill, "This kid's on fire and I think he has potential. Can't you cut him some slack?" Ross witnessed the spark in Bill and took on the role of advocate. With help, Bill eventually took the risk of stepping out of his previous spiritual poverty and loser mentality into something unknown and found success, Purpose, and his true identity in the process. Sometimes risk holds incredibly huge rewards.

Bill Strickland demonstrates how advisors, mentors, and a community can provide opportunities that allow you to escape a poverty of spirit, understand and realize your potential, devise alternate strategies to achieve your goals, and gain the insight and confidence to spot and take smart risks. Every success story reveals the contribution of someone who understood, who knew the person's potential and helped them reach their goals, sometimes in a small way that opened a door they had not seen or did not know existed.

Johnson & Johnson's Story

Executives at Johnson & Johnson faced terrible unexpected scenarios in 1982 and 1986 following the death of eight people due to Tylenol capsules laced with cyanide. Faced with the threat of the loss of a good reputation, the company took a responsible stance and recalled the product from the shelves. In so doing they sustained a loss of $100,000,000. Responding to this catastrophe Johnson and

Johnson developed and pioneered tamper resistant packaging and reintroduced Tylenol in the form of caplets. They became a market leader and have consistently won awards such as "Most Admired Pharmaceutical Company" and "Best Corporate Reputation." Their willingness to investigate to the root causes of a problem to gain a solid understanding of its origin and to seek both short and long-term solutions, once the acute stage of the crisis had passed, constituted an effective risk management approach that involved considerable uncertainty. Taking that big a loss of assets was an enormous risk, but was worth it in view of the long-term reputation of the company. If they failed to regain their solid reputation, they would have been lost in the marketplace and the company would most likely have gone under.

Fear is what stops most of us from taking risks, even smart risks. Susan Jeffers author of *Feel the Fear and Do It Anyway*, points out that she has never heard a mother call out to the child as he or she goes off to school, "Take a lot of risks today, darling." More likely, she says, "Be careful, darling." This early orientation predisposes us to be wary of the world and doubt that we can meet the challenges or take the risks to fully grow. Jeffers points out that she had grown up waiting for fear to go away, playing the when/then game. You know it well. When *this* happens, *then* I will be able to do that. The "when," of course, never happens.

Message to the Reader

There are four main fears that tend to stop us from taking risk:

- Fear of rejection
- Fear of failure
- Fear of what others will think
- Fear of discomfort.

We have already discussed rejection and failure earlier in this chapter related to navigating obstacles. If we learn to reframe rejection and failure as opportunities for learning and growth instead of confirmation of our incompetence, we will help discharge the emotion of fear from the idea of being rejected or failing.

The fear of what others will think is an insidious threat to self-discovery and Living on Purpose, because it implies that we value what others think more than we value what *we* think and feel is right for us. It subtly short-circuits our own personal empowerment and places power over our own lives in the hands of others.

The fear of discomfort is another insidious one. When we get too comfortable, especially in our habits of thinking, speaking, values, and beliefs, we get mired in a rut of tired habits that gets deeper and more entrenched the longer we allow the condition to continue. This rut, our comfort zone, has a narcotic effect on us. We become lulled into believing that we will be happier if we don't do anything to upset the comfort we experience. Facing growth feels uncomfortable because the outcome is unknown. Facing risk feels uncomfortable for the same reason. Pretty soon our zone narrows to the point of disallowing any risk, any growth, and we are drugged by the narcotic effect into believing this is happiness. This is the cost of too much caution and the need to stay comfortable. Sitting on your laurels, accepting the status quo, is the same thing as staying where you are, as we mentioned in Chapter 1, and actually results in going backward in an evolving world—the antithesis of Living on Purpose.

Growth can only happen if we are willing to risk stretching the boundaries that have held us in. Stretching the boundaries of our comfort zones expands and hardens our courage levels. If we never risk, we will never find out what we can do. If we never risk, we will never achieve our dreams. If we never risk, we will never find out that we are much more than we ever dared to dream. If we never risk, we will never find our greatness or our divinity.

In these pages we have offered many tools that are effective in reducing or removing fear. In Chapter 3 we talked about symbolic action, an action, such as parasailing or rock climbing, that we take in a controlled environment specifically for the purpose of stretching our comfort zones or overcoming a particular fear. Having a solid, well-thought-out plan is an effective deterrent to the crippling fears of rejection or failure. Knowing we have steps to take in the direction of our visions and dreams alleviates fear. The vision we hold of our dreams provides the focus by which we can break through the boards of fear as we learned in the segment on board breaking. Self-knowledge—of our strengths, of our inner most identity, of our dreams, of our Purpose—precludes fear. We are now going to arm you further with steps to determine whether a given risk is a smart one or not.

There is never a good time to take a foolhardy risk. A foolhardy risk is one that was not thought out. The potential consequences are not weighed against the potential gain. The likelihood of failure is not considered. The outcome is never examined. But smart risks have passed a rigorous inquiry that assesses the potential for and likelihood of devastating loss.

The final decision will be up to you, of course, but this is a case where the diverse perspectives and input of your trusted mentors or advisors can be advantageous. Assessing risk is one particularly effective application of the scenario planning strategy we discussed in Chapter 4.

When we take the time to examine the potential of a given risk, we determine whether taking it would be a smart move to make or not.

The following are some of the questions that will help you determine the merits of a particular risk:

- What strengths do you and/or your team possess that will help assure success?
- What do you stand to gain by taking the risk?
- What limitations are present in you and/or your team that could deter success?
- What is the worst-case outcome of taking this risk?
- How likely is the worst case to happen?
- Are you prepared to handle the worst case if it happens?
- What is the energy factor? How much energy must you expend to meet the window of opportunity? How likely are you able to mobilize your energy to complete?

If you have limited talents and contributions in a particular situation, you are probably better off not taking the risk unless there are other strong factors that could compensate. If you feel that the worst-case scenario could potentially wipe out your dream entirely, you would want to look *very* closely at your answers to all the other questions before putting your dream at that risk. In some instances, where the potential gain is extraordinary, and the likelihood of the worst-case happening is very small, you would most likely decide to take that risk. It could make a difference if your dream were still in its infancy and not affecting the activities of anyone other than yourself, as opposed to a large operation with many employees depending on you for their income.

In the case of Johnson & Johnson, a security breach resulted in the deaths of some of their customers. The company was looking at risking $100,000,000 to save their reputation, a huge amount of money in anyone's ledger. They stood to regain their good name and standing as a provider of over the counter remedies. Their main liability at the time was the erosion of their reputation and the ticking of the clock that represented their limited window of opportunity. Hesitating or considering their options for too long would negate their final decision in a fickle marketplace. If the effort failed, the worst-case outcome was the crippling or destruction of the business. If they didn't put up the money to help correct the error, the worst-case was very likely to happen. If they failed to act quickly, the worst-case was likely to happen; they didn't have long to deliberate. Johnson & Johnson executives elected to act swiftly, hoping to save the future of the company by putting up a very large amount of money. In this case, risking the future of the company was a smart risk, because if they didn't take the risk, the company would almost certainly, eventually, have failed. The stakes were high enough to warrant taking this risk.

Stories

Nebahat Akkoc's Story

Nebahat's life in southeastern Turkey changed the day her husband Zubeyir was murdered by Kurdish separatists fighting a guerrilla war. The Turkish government denied any connection to his death. Before the murder Nebahat was a primary school teacher; after the murder she became a human rights activist. She was arrested, tortured, and sexually abused by the Turkish police. Through these experiences Nebahat found the inspiration to create Ka-Mer, which means Women's Center.

She imagined a new world: a world in which women have the right to think and act freely, are not polarized, are enriched by various senses of belonging, have the freedom to make their own decisions, a world without hierarchy, discrimination, or violence, where sharing and solidarity are the core, and where people live on the basis of universal human rights without losing their local identity. *http://www.esiweb.org/index.php?lang=en&id=121.*

The principles upon which she founded Ka-Mer were developed to counteract the violence experienced by women within a system built on the basis of violence. Women are defined "as someone's daughter or wife or mother," not as a person in her own right. Nebahat sites this as the root of the violation of the quality of freedom. She states, "Our biggest gain comes from defining the problem as such. We started off not to solve the problem but to understand its roots and dimensions and to accumulate knowledge and experience about ways to resolve it, and then to share this base. We were all victims of violence . . ."

Ka-Mer offers women a safe haven where they might obtain counseling, the raising of consciousness, and a small business loan. A brightly colored arch marks the entrance. All walkways lead to a shaded veranda with a restaurant serving tea and food, offering a respite from the blazing sun. Income from the restaurant and a kindergarten helps support the center's work. Courses teach women about their economic and social rights, where twenty women come together for a ten-week period to discuss topics most of them have never been allowed to discuss. Ninety percent of the women report this is the first time they have talked about many subjects. Economic self-sufficiency is a theme at the center which offers low interest loans to help women start small businesses. Some have opened: a bakery, a greenhouse to grow vegetables, restaurants, a gift box shop, and other small ventures.

A hotline for abused women is also a hotline women who feel their lives are in danger because of the threat of "honor killing," in which a woman is killed by her own family because of a perceived immoral behavior. Ka-Mer offers shelter and medical care, if needed. Although honor killings were made punishable by life imprisonment, women are "locked away in a room with a rope and put under pressure. Or they might be forced to take rat poison," reports Nebahat, in *Time Magazine*.[19] *The San Diego Union Tribune* reported an all-too-common scenario: "Bahar Sogut was fourteen when she shot herself in the head with her father's gun. Her mother and grandmother, who live in a small mud-built house in a Kurdish Muslim village outside Batman in Turkey's poor southeast, said it was her fate." We in Western civilization can't even begin to understand the intense pressure of the mortal danger women in Central Asia and surrounding areas are forced to live with every day.

Nebahat's founding Ka-Mer resulted from the experience of her husband's murder, her own torture, and the increasing awareness of the torture that surrounded her in southeastern Turkey. Her development of entrepreneurial programs followed an increasing awareness that the key to women claiming their personal power, once the abuse was stopped, involved economic empowerment.

Nebahat, named European Social Entrepreneur of the Year, October 30th, 2008, in Istanbul, Turkey, by the World Economic Forum on Europe and Central Asia, founded Ka-Mer in 1997 to promote social and political change, offering entrepreneur programs for women to empower themselves through ownership of small businesses. Currently established in all twenty-three provinces of Eastern and Southeastern Anatolia, Ka-Mer has reached 40,000 women through its educational programming and has provided legal, psychological, and social support for 3,000 women facing domestic violence.[20]

Message to the Reader

Nebahat exemplifies enormous courage in her commitment to taking action in a world where her life was in danger every step of the way. She saw conditions for women so deplorable that she could not allow

---

[19] *http://www.time.com/time/magazine/article/0,9171,1198870,00.html.*
[20] Nebahat decided to change her world by writing a new story. That she succeeded in taking action in the direction of her dream is a miracle. *http://www.weforum.org/en/media.*

it to continue without doing something about it, and this became her dream, her vision of a better world. Nebahat wanted to contribute to the writing of a new story. She saw the biggest liability as lack of financial opportunity for women in her culture. Her courage was strong enough to allow her to take action, in the face of incredible opposition, to correct the liability. Nebahat recognized a larger identity than her culture wanted to give her and her sisters, and found that identity within herself. We couldn't have found a more fitting story to illustrate the larger lessons of these pages. Nebahat said, "Enough is enough," and took measures to begin changing her world, even at the risk of death. It was a risk someone had to take if conditions were ever to begin to change in her world.

Nebahat might not have known what the elements of alignment are. She certainly had never heard the term in the context we have offered in these pages. Worry about rejection or failure didn't exist, nor concern of what others in her culture would think. Fear didn't stop her. For Nebahat, the risk was a smart one, because conditions as they were could not be allowed to continue. She looked inside and found tremendous courage to act in alignment with a self she believed was there—a self who was worthy of respect and opportunity despite her gender—even if no one else in her environment agreed.

Mother Teresa said, "Vision without action is dreaming. Action without vision is drudgery. But vision with action is what miracles are made of." These are the synchronicities, serendipities, and opportunities we have promised since the first chapter. A Life on Purpose is about choosing consciously, with determination and volition, a path of aligned action as we interact with our outer world and make our contribution to it. Mother Teresa understood that aligned action is the stuff from which miracles arise.

Intent into Action
Tools for Chapter 6: Strategies for Aligned Action

When it is time to begin taking action toward your new story, alignment is the most powerful tool in your box. Consistently returning to a state of agreement between your thoughts, words, decisions, actions, beliefs, emotions, values, self-image (your perception of you), and your true core identity (the unchanging you) will give you integrity and congruence—which will in turn attract synchronicity, serendipity, and new opportunities to you. The minutes you spend to evaluate and adjust your focus and alignment will be the most valuable time of the entire day.

When things are not going as you would like, look to see where you are out of alignment with your true self. Is it your thoughts? Your beliefs? Are your words saying something contradictory to your true identity? Does your self-image need updating to match your dream? Are you hanging onto a value from your old patterns?

Getting in alignment involves creating and practicing thoughts, words, beliefs, etc. that will serve your desired trajectory better than the old ones. Beliefs are habits of thought you hold with emotion. To change beliefs, practice new patterns of thought—thoughts that serve you better—and add the emotion of positive anticipation to them. To change values, think all the way through where your old value will take you if you don't change that priority in your life. Then decide on a more productive value, and practice using the new value in determining your priorities. Your words will begin to change when your thinking does. To practice new habits of thinking and speaking, replace an unproductive thought every time you begin to think or say it with a more productive one. If you train yourself to listen to your thoughts and words, you will catch the unproductive ones more often, giving you the opportunity to replace them with the thoughts that serve you better. With practice, the new habits will become second nature to you.

When the new habits come naturally to you, you will find ways to navigate around or through obstacles as they appear, you will have confidence in assessing the merits of a particular risk, you will handle rejection and failure, and you will minimize the negative effects of stress in your life. Better thinking habits will begin to create positive elements that accompany a Life lived on Purpose: passion, inspiration, wisdom, vitality, expansion, and awareness.

The process of aligned action is about evaluating your existing focus and practicing more productive new habits. Your words, beliefs, emotions, values, and decisions all start with a thought; change your thinking and your story will change.

- *Listen to yourself (or ask someone who knows you well) to get an idea of how your words, thoughts, etc. might be contradictory to your true core identity—your greatness.*

- *For every limiting and unproductive thought you notice, create a replacement thought that is more in line with who you REALLY are.*

- *Practice the new thought by replacing the unproductive one with it every time you catch yourself beginning the limiting thought (or word, belief, value, emotion, etc.).*

- *Constantly reevaluate as you gain in experience and awareness.*

7

Leadership and Living on Purpose

*Self-respect cannot be hunted. It cannot be purchased. It is never
for sale. It cannot be fabricated out of public relations. It comes to
us when we are alone, in quiet moments, in quiet places, when we
suddenly realize that, knowing the good, we have done it; knowing the
beautiful, we have served it; knowing the truth, we have spoken it.*

—ALFRED WHITNEY GRISWOLD (27 OCTOBER 1906–19 APRIL 1963) WAS AN
AMERICAN HISTORIAN, WHO WAS PRESIDENT OF YALE UNIVERSITY, 1950–1963.

Wisdom

Our journey in these pages began with the hope found in writing *a new story* for a world
in crisis. We learned that Wisdom consists of integrated knowledge, both conscious and
unconscious. Wisdom is a deep understanding and realizing of people, things, events or situations, resulting in the ability to choose or act to consistently produce the optimum results
with a minimum of time and energy. It is the ability to optimally (effectively and efficiently)

apply perceptions and knowledge and so produce the desired results. Wisdom is also the comprehension of what is true or right coupled with optimum judgment as to action.

A world based on a new story is possible because individuals can choose to rebuild their private world with compassionate values of mutual respect as the basis, and by the ripple effect, as described by Maria's grandfather in Chapter 3, can spread outward, eventually affecting the whole. It begins with individuals looking inward for a better way. As individuals find their stride and implement enlightened change in their personal experiences, they will be looked to for leadership in a world searching for new solutions.

Stories

Joseph Jaworski's Story, Part II

Joe Jaworski founded the American Leadership Forum after his wife left him unexpectedly in 1975, and he decided that leadership in America needed new direction on the heels of Watergate, as told in Chapter 2. This remarkable man was deeply influenced by his inside knowledge of the Watergate cover-up through his father, Leon Jaworski, the Watergate Special Prosecutor. The need for more enlightened leadership was a critical one in Jaworski's mind. He understood that we can't get to a brighter future using historical systems of thought and values.

The following is an excerpt from a book review of Jaworski's *Synchronicity: The Inner Path of Leadership,* by BKConnection.com:

Jaworski describes three fundamental shifts of mind necessary for the creative leadership that will solve some of the world's tougher dilemmas:

1) A shift from resignation to a sense of possibility that comes from seeing the universe as a magical dance, full of living qualities rather than a linear, logical, and predictable view of what's really going on.

2) A shift from seeing ourselves as separate and isolated from everything else that we see 'out there' to seeing the world holistically as a web of relationships. Change one small thing and everything else is subtly different.

3) A shift in the nature of our commitment from a highly disciplined proposition in which you 'seize fate by the throat and do whatever it takes to succeed' to a deeper level of commitment that comes from an [sic] willing spirit. This sense of willingness opens us up to connect with our inner guidance systems and wisdom: to hear the call, to recognize an innate sense of purpose, and to accept and honor that.

"As these shifts occur, we will notice that synchronicity comes into our life, both the personal and the professional. Synchronicity is defined by Carl Jung as 'a meaningful coincidence of two or more events, where something other than the probability of chance is involved.' When synchronicity comes into our life, it's an indication that we are on the path. There is a sense of ease and excitement, a sense of true belonging to ourself [sic], to one another, to the times in which we live, and to life."

In an interview reported by Alan M. Webber (*Fast Company*, "Destiny and the Job of the Leader," June 30, 1996), Jaworski reveals more of his impressive depth of understanding of enlightened leadership.

AMW: In business, what is the job of the leader?

JJ: Leadership is discovering the company's destiny and having the courage to follow it.

AMW: Do you believe that companies have destinies?

JJ: Yes, I do. But it's not the same thing as a company vision. A company's destiny is a matter of purpose, an expression of why it exists. I think we're beginning to understand that companies that endure have a noble purpose.

AMW: How is your definition of leadership different from the more traditional definition?

JJ: Most leadership programs begin with a description of the attributes of the leader—a leader has vision, a leader has courage, a leader inspires others. All of that's fine; it's very important. But what's leadership really all about? To me, leadership is a journey toward wholeness. A leader's journey starts by looking inward to understand, Why am I here? What is it that I'm here to do?

AMW: The traditional notion of leadership is that it's about leading others. You're saying it's about discovering yourself.

JJ: Before you can lead others, before you can help others, you have to discover yourself. Today a leader can't impose himself on others. He makes himself available to others. And nothing is more powerful than someone who knows who they are.

Once you can be that way, all those other wonderful traits flow from that. They become apparent. Authenticity—if you know what you're all about and where you're heading, you become more authentic. Credibility—if you know who you are, then people trust you.

The traditional view of leadership talks about leadership as a package, but it looks at the outside of the package. I'm talking about starting with what's inside the package.

AMW: David Bohm, the world-famous physicist, had a powerful impact on your thinking. What did you learn from him?

JJ: David Bohm was a brilliant scientist, a colleague of Einstein. He was also the most spiritual being I've ever met. He taught me a fundamentally different way of looking at the world.

What he told me was that there was an order underneath the reality that most of us live in; he called it the 'implicate order.' One of the deepest assumptions of humans is that we can't really make choices, that reality is what it is. But Bohm believed that if we're truly in touch with the implicate order, we can sense what will happen and participate in making it manifest. If we reach deeply into ourselves, we will be able to discover what's going to happen and participate in bringing it forth.

AMW: How does that relate to business strategy?

JJ: The work I did at Royal Dutch/Shell in scenario planning was some of the most advanced planning that business does. We created a very sensitive approach to listening and discovering the directions that events were moving in. But we were still reactive. We were waiting for events to unfold, and then seeking to respond as quickly as we could.

David Bohm's insight taught me that there's something even more profound than scenario planning. It's strategy where you go inside the implicate order to sense what wants to happen and then participate in guiding and nudging it along.

AMW: How can businesses apply your view of leadership and strategy?

JJ: Everybody in business today understands the need to transform their companies. This is particularly true in big companies. But they also understand that the things we've tried don't go far enough. Techniques like reengineering have been discredited. I believe that the way to transform a company begins with personal transformation. And the way to personal transformation begins with the kind of leadership I'm talking about.

I believe that the top leadership group in a company has to commit itself to a journey of self-discovery. And the leaders have to provide space for the other people in the company to do the same. If you want a creative explosion to take place, if you want the kind of performance that leads to truly exceptional results, you have to be willing to embark on a journey that leads to an alignment between an individual's personal values and aspirations and the company's values and aspirations.

Leaders like Joe Jaworski are needed in the world. His depth of insight is inspiring. Jaworski suggests that vision and dreams are not the deepest core of our relationship with the outer world. What he calls "destiny" (of a company) equates directly to what we have described as "Purpose" on an individual level. It is the expression of your concept of "self" into the world through your work. Purpose suggests an expression that is innate, that we have prepared for our entire lives, that draws upon every talent and ability we possess, that is unique to each one of us, and that allows expression of our heritage. Our dreams and our visions of them happening are not the ultimate goal, rather they are the means, the vehicle, by which we explore our Purpose.

*I believe the way to transform
a world begins with personal
transformation.*

Jaworski says that this is a journey toward wholeness, of looking inward to understand why we are here. He suggests that knowing what we are about and where we're heading will result in authenticity. Joe Jaworski says that he believes that the way to transform a company begins with personal transformation.

Jaworski sees transformation happening in the corporate landscape from the top down, certainly the most efficient way for it to come about. But because transformation is an individual event, it can also be implemented from whatever level individuals happen to occupy during the time of their personal transformation. Remember the power of the ripple effect. We do not need to wait upon the motivation of our hierarchy to begin individual self-discovery and transformation. Transformation of what? Of our relationship with ourselves and with each other, of our discovery of and connection to our core identities, of the priorities that shape our lives, of the way we think, the way we feel, the words we speak, and of the way we view the world, how it works, and our position in it.

How will the world change as the shifts Jaworski saw as fundamental in solving some of the tougher dilemmas begin to occur? Every individual who shifts from resignation to a sense of possibility will experience enhanced physical, emotional, and mental energy, hope, and a sense of positive expectation that will result in creating expansive levels of energy. This will begin to pave the way for opportunities and synchronicities that could not have come about prior to the shift. Life becomes more fun when we perceive expanded possibility, more of an adventure. When possibilities exist, life becomes more secure and less random.

When we shift from seeing ourselves as separate to seeing the world holistically, as a web of relationships affected by what each one does, we will recognize we do not have to do it all alone. A spirit of shared community and cooperative effort would begin to rise along with greater respect for differences between individuals, races, and cultures. A sense of "us" as in "all of us" would begin to replace "us vs. them" and the taking of entrenched, opposing sides.

A shift from the belief that we must "make it happen by whatever means necessary" to the willingness to accept inner guidance and wisdom would result in the spread of peace of mind and a sense of Purpose in Life. Urgency and desperation would give way to confidence and patience. The belief that there can be only one winner and everyone else loses would be replaced with the idea that everyone can and should win in the game of life and work; highest benefits would not be exclusive to the special few. Fear would fade away to be replaced with confidence.

These are a few of the potential gains from the shifts Jaworski talks about in his book. The implications are deep and far-reaching. They all can be realized by the courageous individuals who choose to take a path of self-examination and discovery, who choose to pursue a Life on Purpose. It is a shift from a focus on the outside of the package that Jaworksi mentioned, the old story focus, to looking at what's on the inside of the package, the focus of the new story.

We have given a great deal of attention to alignment. Jaworski suggests that the role of leadership in the workplace is to "embark on a journey that leads to an alignment between an individual's dreams and aspirations and the company's dreams and aspirations," and pave the way to an explosion of creativity leading to truly exceptional results. He gets the concept of not just alignment, but the alignment between individuals and the companies they work for. As we explained in an earlier chapter that the combined strengths of individuals become the strengths of the team, so is there a need for agreement (alignment) between the dreams and aspirations of both the individuals and the company or organization they comprise. This is a new dimension in leadership.

Responsibility and Personal Power

We have talked in previous chapters about responsibility. What that means is taking responsibility for your own future, not relying on historical patterns, the conditions of the world economy, or the whims of individuals you hope will hire you. It is about directing your own life, your own path, with determination and volition rather than accepting and reacting to what happens by default. It is about creating a place for yourself that allows full self-expression and discovery. It is about honoring and respecting yourself enough to give yourself permission to shine and thus to give others permission to do the same. It is about reclaiming the power that is rightfully yours. It is about living the life you were meant to live: finding and engaging your greatness through your work—a Life on Purpose. It is the ultimate responsibility, the most rewarding and the most fulfilling.

Responsibility and personal power go hand in hand. To refuse responsibility is to relinquish your power. To refuse your power is to abandon responsibility. Through deciding you will write your own story and through being responsible for it, you cause the doorway to power to open.

Power belongs to whoever is responsible for the impact.

Responsibility has to be in place before you can initiate change. If you can't accept responsibility for the impact you have on your world, how can you expect to make a conscious impact upon your future circumstances? This is the relationship between responsibility and power.

Transition to Greatness and Leadership

Our journey has been about transitions: from one job to the next, from one career to the next, from a thought to a dream to a reality, from reactive to deliberate, from victim to creator, from fear to courage, from avoidance to responsibility, from the old story into the new story, from lack of meaning to Purpose. Whatever your specific transitions, we have sought to provide pragmatic, useful information that takes the deeper messages from theory into the realm of everyday practicality. Unless we can apply theory in daily living, it is empty words no matter how lofty or beautiful.

As you progress in your journey of self-discovery, you will transition from a follower to a leader. This is true whether your dream is to build an international organization or to simply upgrade your relationship with your current job. As you gain confidence in your personal identity, people will begin to look to you for creative perspectives. Discovering and engaging your inherent greatness will propel you into a role of leadership by the example you embody in how you interact with yourself, your life, and your world.

In studying "The architecture of human greatness" Parameshwar Srikantia found that "Greatness, it appears, is like an oasis that human beings retreat to in order to uphold their humanity, persevere with their most cherished ideals, and maintain their integrity regardless of the trouble and tribulations that the external world may impose on them." Pursuing a Life of Purpose opens the door to expose our greatness.

Focusing on the pursuit of your dream and what it contributes to the world opens you to an expanding awareness of your Purpose. Living a Life on Purpose offers you layers of remembering more and more of who you are and who you might become. It is this remembrance that will allow you to bring forth the reality of your dream, your Purpose, and your divinity. **Never doubt the value of your unique contribution. You make a difference for yourself and for all of us.** No one else can bring forth what you can—your greatness—emerging out of your unique combination of passion, strengths, experiences, and dreams.

Embracing and expressing our greatness in the arena of our work is the wise interaction from our innermost core with our outside world. To get there, we have examined the wisdom inherent in the functioning of our cells. We have presented examples through the stories of a variety of everyday people who have something valuable to teach us. We have drawn upon our own life experience and have attempted to look beyond historical patterns of thought for new ideas and creative perspectives that integrate the wisdom we have encountered.

Embracing our greatness involves self-discovery, personal responsibility for our words and actions, and focus on our strengths, true identity, and Purpose. It involves maintaining alignment so that we function in congruence with our dreams and our essence.

Alignment has the power to lay the old story to rest and take us successfully toward a brighter, more enlightened future.

Without alignment, we are dressing up the old story in new words and are NOT affecting sustainable, positive evolutionary change. Authentic leadership is about living in alignment and leading *by example* from a foundation of self-knowledge.

Authenticity comes from connection with the deepest core and from living without armor, without masks, without pretense, without the need for peer approval.

The authentic leader looks for and transcends the problems to find new creative perspectives. The authentic leader uses feedback as an invaluable reality check.

Cellular Wisdom at Work

Feedback is essential to the optimal functioning within cells and between cells in tissues, organs, and systems. Complex networks of feedback, such as those that involve the brain, the pituitary, and the testes or ovary, ensure reproductive competence. Feedback promotes optimal functioning by providing information required to continually monitor and adjust the beating of the heart, the tension in the muscles, blood glucose, and a host of other critical functions. Without feedback homeostasis, the regulation of the internal environment of the body, could not occur. This regulation allows us to function in a wide range of external environments.

The importance of receiving feedback is evidenced in the fact that the membranes that surround every cell are literally filled with receptors, specialized molecules, to receive all sorts of information.

Cells create receptors that will bring information relevant to the nature of the cell. For example, neurons that receive information from a specific neurotransmitter, such as serotonin, will have receptors for that molecule. If the neuron does not need information from a different neurotransmitter, such as acetylcholine, it will not have receptors for that molecule. Cells stay true to their nature and ignore irrelevant information.

The body's message is clear: feedback is appropriate to the cell type and is coupled to action. It is the nature of feedback to result in adjustments, specifically adjustments that are appropriate to the nature of the cell.

The body demonstrates the importance of continual feedback and adjustment. This information is indispensable because it provides a measure of the impact of our actions on others. Sometimes the information represents a startling perspective. Ignoring such information could lead to the demise of your dream.

Message to the Reader

Most of us recoil from the prospect of receiving disparate or critical information. Yet this avoidance could be fatal to one's career, business, or profession, as it precludes the ability to make needed adjustments indicated by such information.

Openness constitutes the foundation of authentic leadership, including openness to discrepant information, without denying its reality. Only then can you adequately address the issue, the essence of taking responsibility.

Opening to a wide range of information regarding the impact of your leadership remains the most comprehensive strategy to appraise your effectiveness as a leader. Feedback provides the opening conversation for taking responsibility.

Bill Gates reminds us that "You need to know about customer feedback that says things should be better." Have you ever eaten at a restaurant with poor food and/or poor service? Didn't you want to offer some insight from the consumer who keeps their doors open about how they could improve business by improving the quality of the food and the service? Usually, if we say anything, the suggestions are met with defensiveness or indifference, so we tend to keep our opinions to ourselves. But in many cases the survival of the business is in danger. As the employee, manager, or owner, wouldn't you be smart to put personal feelings aside and *listen* to such feedback? The aligned leader realizes that he or she may need input to point out areas of blindness as well as ways to improve the business, product, or job being done.

> *Criticism means that you need to take a hard look at how you are going about doing what you are doing, at the quality you are or are not delivering.*

If your food is good, if your product is good, if your service is good, and the timing is right, you *will* have a demand for your product or service. If you notice demand slowing down or not catching on, use that fact as feedback in itself. Lack of enthusiasm for your product or service means you are missing the mark somewhere, assuming, of course, that people know about your product or service. (This applies equally to job applicants—if you are not having success getting hired, perhaps where you are missing the mark is on your true calling, perhaps you are still trying to play too small, perhaps you are avoiding your true, deepest Purpose.)

- The product or service is offered in an oversaturated or poorly timed market
- The customer had a less than stellar experience when they tried it out
- The product or service is not of high enough excellence to warrant coming back for more

If your product happens to be your own competence, offered to an employer, it is up to you to deliver excellence in what you do. Mediocrity and barely getting by will not move you into a wealth of opportunities; it is in the quest for excellence that you will encounter more of who you are and bring forth more of your greatness. It is also in the quest for excellence that your product or service will have its best chance for success. Every idea you come in contact with, no matter the source of the feedback, if it expands your product or service or if it enhances the quality, is invaluable to you. The more welcoming you are of constructive feedback, the more you will receive and benefit.

Maria's Story

When we left Maria in Chapter 5, she had successfully completed her open house and hired Elizabeth and Samantha to help meet the production deadline resulting from the open house showcase. In the meantime, Maria has completed the transition from part time cashier to full time jewelry designer and producer. Over the months that followed, Maria was introduced to a teacher who has helped Maria learn about aligned action. Maria realized that she would not have been open to learning these principles in her old state of mind, emotion, and beliefs. But because her grandfather helped her find hope for changing her experience in her world, previously closed doors inside her began to open, and as she learned more about herself and what she was capable of, doors continued to open for her.

Maria shared her knowledge of aligned action with John and her employees. Having a common goal of alignment and continuing self-discovery has bonded the team together in ways that surprise and delight them each on a daily and weekly basis. They serve each other as reminders of what they are working toward and the alignment they all seek to maintain. They are not perfect in their alignment, but they pause to acknowledge and appreciate every step forward any of them make and find humor in their unsuccessful attempts. On tough days there is always someone who helps bring back a positive focus. Maria has had the thought that it might be time to start looking for their next team member, a part-time sales person.

She is driving across town to attend a monthly class with her teacher. Traffic is heavy. It's been a busy and trying day. Maria turns on the radio for some relaxing music to help realign her various aspects and she feels her mind grow quiet and still. Safeway appears on her right, and she turns into the parking lot. She doesn't know why she turns, she just does. She parks, goes into the grocery store, and finds herself on the bread aisle. Again, she had not been thinking that she needed bread, she just goes there. She remembers that she actually does need a loaf of bread and reaches for the kind she likes. A lady next to her turns to see if her shopping cart is in Maria's way. She and Maria recognize each other. "Maria?" "Helen!" They laugh at running into each other in the bread aisle. Helen is a long-time friend of Maria's mother.

"How's the jewelry business going?" asks Helen. "Didn't I hear your mother mention that you are making a business out of your jewelry hobby?"

"It's going great," Maria answers. "I'm so glad to see you here, Helen, of all places. We are just beginning to think about looking for a part time sales person. Haven't you had some experience in sales?"

"You know, I have had. Since Jack retired I've been looking for an excuse to get out of the house more. We're driving each other crazy. Would fifteen years of selling insurance be the kind of experience you would need? I just wouldn't be able to commit to very many hours a week right now. What are you looking for?"

"Not too many hours a week and someone who knows how to sell," Maria mirrors Helen's words with a broad grin. They exchange phone numbers and e-mail addresses and promise to call soon. Helen goes back to her shopping and Maria pays for her bread before continuing on her way to class. She can't believe her good fortune. Not only did she get out of traffic, but she remembered she needed a loaf of bread, *and* she might have found their sales rep!

Maria tells her teacher about the interesting experience she had. The teacher brightens and responds: "That's intuition. Good job!"

Maria knows that with all she is learning, her business is going to do well. She knows that she is much better prepared to meet the challenges of navigating her life as it relates to her work. In just a few short months she has transitioned from someone who could do nothing but complain about her job to someone in charge of her own future. She knows much, much more about herself and who she is. She is both proud of and humbled by her knowledge of her true self. She is so filled with gratitude for the blossoming of her self-discovery that fills her with great joy. All she can think to do is to share the wonder with everyone she meets.

Message to the Reader

Our choice is whether to follow these impressions or not. If Maria had hesitated, missed the opportunity to turn into Safeway, and had decided to keep going, she would have missed the synchronistic meeting with Helen. She would have had to take all the normal steps in hiring: deciding together with John exactly what the new role would be, advertising, answering calls about the ad, setting up interviews, talking with each applicant, etc. Following the intuitive impulse allowed Maria to skip over all those steps. Now she only has to do the process of qualifying Helen's balance sheet and personality style, if they decide to complete that process. John and Maria might decide to take the intuitive impression plus Helen's years as an insurance salesperson as adequate qualification.

"Intuition (is) perception via the unconscious."
—*Carl Gustav Jung*

So you start your day by reviewing the status of ongoing projects and the energy required to do the next steps. You decide on a strategy for accomplishing a task. During the process, you suddenly feel strongly that you need to look up the phone number of someone you haven't thought of in years. Before you get a chance to find the number, your sister calls and says she was thinking about the person you were going to look at and would you come to dinner the next evening? You say you will come and you finish the day's task. On the way home on the radio news there is a story about someone with the same name you were going to look up, the person you and your sister both thought of. The next afternoon, following a moment of mental quiet, you leave your office and go into the parking lot of the building next door (you just go—**intuition**) only to find the individual you and your sister were thinking about getting out of his car to go into a meeting next door. After you both get over your surprise at the "coincidence," you chat for a few moments and discover that the individual has the missing piece of information that solves a challenge you have been dealing with at work. When you get to dinner at your sister's house, she mentions that she has been trying to solve the very same challenge but had never mentioned it to you previously.

In this example, events seem to lead from one to the next, but it won't always happen that way. There is no road map; there is no manual. All we can do is present some scenarios that illustrate how intuition can lead you along the road. This will add a new dimension to your information-gathering process, and it is invaluable to develop a working awareness of it.

Wise Decisions

Shifting from the role of service provider, manufacturer of goods, or link in the chain of personnel under another leader, you will find yourself spending more of your time making decisions. Making wise decisions, using knowledge to make decisions with love, will distinguish your new path from the old story as you transition into a role of greater leadership.

How does one use wisdom in making decisions? Remember in Chapter 5 when we cautioned about hiring a friend for the wrong reasons? Do you realize it would not be wise to hire that friend, even though they need a job? In this example, you consider what is best for the company. It would never jeopardize the well-being of the venture, the dream, by having an unproductive drain on the financial resources; it would respect the friend enough to know they need to find a situation that suits them, their strengths, and their particular form of competence; the most wise decision would honor that friend enough to be honest with them and kind enough to deliver your decision gently and with tact. **Wisdom seeks the best advantage and outcome for every individual involved**. It will seek the solution that gives the best opportunity for everyone to win, not just a few. The health of the venture must be nurtured and protected just as carefully as one would want to nurture and protect team members. If you don't protect the venture, it won't be in a position to offer anyone anything.

You might ask how it is an advantage for the friend to not be hired by your company. Keep in mind that every employer/employee relationship needs to be the best fit possible of the company's needs with the unique strengths of the applicant. A win on both sides of the table constitutes a good match. If your friend (or relative) is not the right match for your needs, he or she will not be making the best use of their strengths and thus will not have the opportunity for their greatest fulfillment in the job, in addition to not offering the mix of strengths your position needs. This is the difference between making a decision that seems to make sense (hiring a friend who needs a job) and making a *wise* decision that includes consideration of the whole regardless of what others will think of you for making it.

Difficult decisions will be easier when made from a solid foundation of self-knowledge, alignment of Purpose, and focus on the end result. It is wiser to make the desired end result about expanded opportunities for growth and self-discovery than about personal gain or glory.

Beware of the trap of second-guessing yourself once you have made a decision. Let go of the process after the decision is made. If you continue to examine the pros and cons, wonder whether you made the right choice, or doubt your decision, you undermine your personal power. Second-guessing keeps you from moving forward and chokes your supply of energy just as surely as avoidance of making a given decision. Try it when you are having a hard time deciding what to do about something. Let the process ramble on for a while. Notice how diluted and dispersed your energy becomes. Once you notice that, make a decision with the awareness of wisdom and don't let yourself second-guess it. It is your decision and you are standing firm in it. You will discover that the decision itself is not nearly as critical as getting clear inside about the fact that the deed is done and it's time to move on to other things. This relates directly to the principles of making and announcement and commitment discussed in Chapter 2. The act of committing to a given decision frees your creative energy for forward movement. Avoiding the announcement or commitment diffuses, dilutes, and stalls your creative energy. Second-guessing your decision after making it equates to not having actually made a commitment to the decision, and leaves your creative energy diffused and stuck.

Winston Churchill's Story

Stories

Winston Churchill provides an exemplary model of responsibility and raw personal courage in the face of many challenges: a childhood lisp, absence of parental love, lack of a formal college education, political challenges and defeats, loss of a child, and personal battles with depression. Criticized for being an intuitive decision maker, his predictions of two world wars and the cold war were appreciated only after the fact.

When Churchill no longer had a Cabinet position, he could not abandon his vision for Britain's welfare and ultimate survival. He chose a route of high risk, comments Larry Kryske in his book *The Churchill Factors: Creating Your Finest Hour*(Trafford Publishing, 2006). He had the courage to warn his country. He took a stand and never gave in.

Churchill knew that an alliance with America was essential to winning the war. He needed to create a personal relationship with Franklin D. Roosevelt in spite of the fact that there was strong support in the U.S. for America to remain separate and apart from the war. Attempting to create this personal relationship with FDR entailed significant risk. Churchill did not know FDR well enough to know if he would honor his requests, particularly in light of reports, such as those sent by Joseph Kennedy, predicting Britain's defeat by Nazi Germany. Churchill communicated candidly with FDR, which required courage considering the circumstances and the differences of opinion they held. Churchill risked negative public opinion at home to forge an alliance with America. Kryske reports that in the five years between 1939 and 1945, Churchill sent FDR over 1,100 letters and telegrams, in addition to their ten or more in-person meetings. It is not overstating his importance to say that Churchill's decisions to risk others' opinions of him led to the resolution of world wars. As Churchill states: "The price of greatness is responsibility."

For Winston Churchill, his willingness to take an unpopular position in view of what he considered his larger responsibility to his country and the world was the foundation of his historic greatness. Even though he spent many years in politics, popularity was trivial for him in view of what he determined he needed to do. We can see how interrelated taking responsibility is with evoking greatness. There is also a strong connection between greatness and refusing to give up on the vision, particularly in view of the bigger picture—how the vision relates to the world at large. And for that vision to have an impact, as Churchill so well understood, it must be effectively communicated to others.

Cellular Wisdom at Work

 In early simple organisms, such as single cells, little choice prevailed. Should a stimulus come along that was sensed to be harmful, movement quickly ensued. As more complicated organisms emerged, the possible responses to a single stimulus increased. In the human body more than eighty percent of neurons are not involved in direct sensing or movement, but rather in transmitting information initially received by receptors to various parts of the brain and spinal cord. The information interpreted leads to responses such as movement. Extraordinarily astute at distinguishing pertinent information, the body always chooses a response that is most adaptive. **A normal, healthy body continually and consistently communicates its vision to every cell, tissue, organ, and system**.

The authentic leader communicates from a position of alignment, responsibility, and intuition. A powerful vision, communicated by a charismatic leader, evokes emotion. It helps people see their own worth. It inspires and motivates people to implement the change envisioned. The purpose of communicating the vision is to motivate others to take action. This is accomplished in three steps.

Message to the Reader

- First, the vision must be transferred from thought into words
- Second, the words must engage emotion: cooperative purpose, hope, confidence, conviction, contribution
- Third, the emotion must be transformed into action

This has to happen within you before it can be effectively communicated to others. When you act and communicate from a position of the alignment of your thoughts, words, emotions, beliefs, values, and true identity, others will be drawn to the conviction you hold of your Purpose. **Keeping the vision communicated, frequently, helps your team stay motivated and on course with the trajectory you desire.**

Another aspect of communicating as an authentic leader is communicating to your team members and co-workers their value to the endeavor. In her book, *Confidence: How Winning Streaks and Losing Streaks Begin and End* (Crown Business, 2006), Rosabeth Moss Kanter tells the story of the University of Connecticut Huskies women's basketball team's loss to Villanova in the Big East Conference Championship game. This loss ended their seventy-nine-game winning streak. In the locker room after the game, Geno Auriemma, the head coach, asked the players to "look deeply at themselves." He pointed out that they had "stopped caring about one another; they'd stopped making that extra pass; they needed to restore the chemistry of collaboration." Auriemma followed up with meetings calling upon each team member to examine herself and find the strength to recover. He told the team's lead player, Diana Taurasi, and the other two leaders, "We have either one game or six games left. It's up to you. You have to pull together. You have to fix this. It has to be you leading this team." Then he spoke to the freshman, "Now's the time to show why you're here . . . The three of you are going to decide whether we win this tournament, because we can't do it without you . . ." The team went on to win and Taurasi bounced back. Rosabeth Moss Kanter comments that their communication, respect, responsibility, and collaboration was renewed and that with it came the collective strength to meet any challenge. Auriemma's leadership emerged from his vision of members working together in sync, feeding off of each other, and led the team back to be once again a winning one.

In sports, business, or any aspect of joint activity, leading from alignment and vision anchors the reality of the dream that motivates us to action. Remember Mother Teresa's words, ". . . vision with action is what miracles are made of."

Your leadership must reflect the vision at the core of your dream. Any incongruence between your vision and your action will diffuse your credibility and your power. Your ability to influence others depends upon you leading from vision and alignment with all aspects of your true identity. Taking the position as leader demands that you understand your role as leader, including the integral actions and dimensions of that role. As suggested by Rosabeth Moss Kanter:

"Leaders must wake people out of inertia. They must get people excited about something they've never seen before, something that does not yet exist."

Self-Image

The multiple roles of a career entrepreneur, delineated by Amon Brock Eubanks in his dissertation "The Roles and Competencies of Career Entrepreneurs: Implications for Training and Career Development," include:

- Visionary
- Strategic planner
- Manager/leader
- Communicator
- Marketer
- Innovator/inventor
- Financial planner and manager
- Motivator
- Sales person
- Financier
- Human resource director
- Bookkeeper
- Accountant
- Janitor.

Even if you do not plan to become an entrepreneur, leadership intrinsically carries the responsibility for multiple roles. The scope can become overwhelming and will challenge the parameters of your self-image.

While in the past you might have identified yourself with a specific role, that role may have already disintegrated, or will likely disintegrate, as you pursue your new story. A new perspective about who you are brews in the depths of your being, even as you pursue the work that brings fulfillment. As you find your role transitioning into one of leadership, it will be important to keep your self-image up to speed with the changing roles.

We tend to limit ourselves by the image we hold of ourselves: strong and independent, not good at math, good at science, baggy tee shirt and jeans type, pinstripe suit type, easily led by others, mule-headed, incompetent, unworthy, financially poor, opposed to big business, a tycoon, left-wing, right-wing, just a housewife, a frazzled clerk, under-educated, over-qualified, too old, too young, too heavy, too inexperienced . . . the list goes on and on.

Of all the aspects that contribute to the manifestation of our dreams, our sense of who we are and what we think can accomplish is the most potent.

The following are a few examples of more statements to help get your own creative juices flowing.

I am . . .

- Poised for creative action
- Expanding in awareness daily
- The expression of endless possibility
- An authentic and aligned leader
- Worthy of contributing to the new story
- Capable and competent in my field
- Willing and ready to change my personal world
- Confident of my role and place in the larger world
- An integrative tool for enlightened evolution.

You are engaged in a process of creating your Purpose. Whether you are creating a new career, profession, or business or re-engineering the one you already have, you sense a calling to future work that emerges out of your Purpose. The process of creating or re-engineering it is a learning process incorporating the new and releasing what does not work from the old. Trusting the process gives you the freedom to explore, assess and determine direction, decision by decision. A part of you already has the deep knowledge of your calling and its potential manifestations. You are not without guidance throughout this process. Quiet solitude and reflection are the portals to access your inner wisdom. Only by checking within as you travel the journey can you ascertain if your decisions follow your calling or lead you astray. If you have fallen off course, stop, listen to your inner guidance, then act on that inner wisdom, self-correcting to bring you back on course.

Realize the cyclic nature of this process, such that you will continually be involved in developing your work to meet the criteria that are important to you. This is not a one-time process, but a dynamic, continual engagement in bringing more and more of your greatness to the world through your work. As you do this, your self-image will need to grow to stay ahead of the new demands.

As you explore the various pieces we have presented together, you will find yourself living from your true self, with a strong sense of who you are, and aligning your actions with your truth.

Cynthia Arey's Story

Stories

Cynthia Arey's journey to authentic leadership involved a re-creation of herself in response to cancer. A successful real estate representative in Richmond, Virginia, Cynthia traveled to Boulder, Colorado, to take an educational program for home owners about how to sell their homes. With this introduction, Cynthia decided to move to Boulder. Three years after she settled in Colorado, Cynthia noticed a lump on her collar bone. It was diagnosed as cancer.

A single woman, Cynthia knew she needed to continue selling real estate even with her illness. She would have to engage in her work with a great deal of what she calls *energy management.* "I would use the least amount of energy in the most refined way to get results," she recounted in my interview with her. Cynthia began her process with a "re-creation notebook." She would note anything which caused her to be angry, fearful, or negative in any way. She said, "I wanted to identify my anger to see how I misused it." Her first phase of her re-creation process involved softening the anger. She would tell herself that this circumstance simply "annoyed" her. In the next phase she used humor. Eventually that same circumstance no longer had an impact on her whatsoever.

How was Cynthia able to do this? "When you get very sick, the reality of your life span becomes clear to you in physical form. I began looking at every sunrise and every sunset. I paused to appreciate the dynamics of things, the squirrel in the yard. I became a lot more respectful of myself, more loving, more appreciative of who I am. Thankfulness, gratitude, humility became part of my life. Anger became hilarious. If you are thankful for living, how can someone cutting you off on the highway be an issue? It made a huge shift in my life."

"In real estate," Cynthia remarked, "you are dealing with the most important emotional and financial investment people make. You get to deal with every issue a person has. They project it into the real estate transaction. I help my clients navigate the process. I empower them."

Cynthia developed a procedure for successfully working with her real estate team, including clients, colleagues, and associates. First, she assesses their personalities. If she sees them as detailed oriented, like an accountant (Chapter 5), she provides them with data. If bottom line people, she gets directly to the point. If they are the generous social type she adds focus to what she does with them. If they are the undecided type, fearful to make a decision she carefully but concisely identifies their options, pointing out the consequences of their decisions. In all cases she lets them decide.

A southern gentleman who once shared Cynthia's office remarked to her one day, "You are like knowing ten different people. You talk one way to the little old lady, another way to the banker, another way to the attorney, another way to the lender, and yet another way to the appraisers." Cynthia does this so that her clients can really hear her and be empowered to make a decision.

Cynthia sustains her thoughts, emotions, and actions at what she refers to as a "high level" to be an anchor for her clients and to provide them an opportunity to step up to that level themselves. If a person other than the decision maker "intercedes in the process and is obstructive," she does not stand by and allow that behavior. For example, a mother who said she really understood real estate brought her daughter to Cynthia as a client. The mother attempted to tell the daughter what she should do. Cynthia asked the mother, "Would you want to decimate the dream of your daughter? What are you choosing to do?" Firm in asking this question, Cynthia helped the mother realize that she was accountable for her actions regarding her daughter. In Cynthia's questioning the mother, she cleared the way for the daughter to make a choice.

Cynthia uses her energy in what she calls "the highest form" to get to the quickest result. While making a presentation to a client, explaining how she was going to market his house and the approach she was going to take selling his house, the client interrupted Cynthia four times asking how much his house was worth. After the fourth interruption, Cynthia closed her notebook. She addressed the client this way. "I think it is better if you communicate with someone who serves your needs. The best thing I can do, now, is leave." Cynthia headed for the door. The man requested that Cynthia come back and sit down, commenting that he would not interrupt her any more. After this interchange, he listened. He was kind. He was polite. Previously, he had his own agenda and would not listen to her. "If they intercede I pull back. I do not try to persuade them. I do not do this in an abusive way. When they are wallowing down there, I tell them I am up here. Are you going to step up?" Throughout the process, she is not offended. As she puts it, if she takes the comments personally and becomes offended, she becomes "susceptible to the muck."

Cynthia attempts to pre-pave and position her clients to reduce their stress in buying a home. She has observed, "When people attach their emotions to the process, it plummets them. They go down fast." When her clients say, "I have to have this house," Cynthia responds with, "Let's change the word to prefer. This house would meet your needs." Intentionally, in softening the words, she helps to reduce their attachment so that if anything goes askew, she does not have to deal with bringing them "back up." She may remark, "This is an amazing house. We will find something else this nice or better." She refers to this as "detaching the attachment."

"I think that for me to be all I can be in the very highest form is what I am about. I bring that into my business. I give people the opportunity to tap into it. They can be all they can be. When we go to the table people are happy. It is a joyful process." This is how Cynthia describes her Purposeful and aligned form of leadership.

Aaron Feuerstein's Story

We were living in Boston when the images of the largest fire Massachusetts had seen for a century, later recognized as among the top ten worse industrial fires ever in the U.S., lit up the TV screen. Although 500 people were working at Malden Mills, no one was killed that December 11, 1995. On December 14, less than two weeks before Christmas, the CEO, Aaron Feuerstein, of the family-owned Lawrence, Massachusetts, manufacturer of Polartec and Polarfleece, assembled his employees in a high school gymnasium. Employees awaited his announcement with anxious anticipation. Contrary to feared expectations, Feuerstein announced to his 3,100 employees that they would be paid their salaries with full benefits, including the traditional Christmas bonus, in spite of the fact that his business was destroyed. Instead of retiring with the insurance money, Feuerstein used the insurance monies to pay the employee salaries and rebuild the factory. Some thought Feuerstein would build the factory in the South or oversees to reduce operating expenses. Instead, he chose to rebuild in the original location in Lawrence. Feuerstein explained in an interview with "Parade Magazine" in 1996, "I have a responsibility to the worker, both blue-collar and white-collar. I have an equal responsibility to the community. It would have been unconscionable to put 3,100 people on the streets and deliver a deathblow to the cities of Lawrence and Methuen. Maybe on paper our company is worthless to Wall Street, but I can tell you it's worth more."

Among the many gifts Feuerstein received from people in Massachusetts and across the U.S., his favorite was a patchwork quilt made from strips of Polartec by Hebrew day school children. The quilt contained the words: "Who is honored? One who honors others."

Reflecting on his actions Feuerstein comments, "...I created the spark, the hope, the will to overcome and salvage a situation that had seemed impossible. I was able to influence others to participate in that dream. Not just by the few words I said that evening. It had to do with a history together of treating human beings as God's creatures—my confidence that they all had a divine spark in them, and that they could all do it."

Cynthia's life threatening disease triggered her purposeful re-creation of herself and her clear engagement in authentic leadership. Today Cynthia's vitality embraces you and you understand how thoroughly she lives. Fortunately, we do not have to face death in order to discover our authentic leadership. The benefits of leading with alignment include not only sustainable success, but a sense of knowing who you are and living from the *inside-out*, consistently, and with great élan and well being.

Message to the Reader

Aaron Feuerstein exemplifies alignment of his values of his responsibilities to his employees and community, his awareness of the human identity—with his actions. His choice to use the insurance settlement money to meet the payroll his employees depended on and to rebuild the company so it could continue to make its contribution in the community tells us that our contribution goes way beyond the product or service we provide. It also encompasses every life we touch: our own, our team, our community. This illustrates beautifully how we are interconnected, as if in a web, affecting others by every step we take.

When you are authentic, aligned, you experience a sense of deep satisfaction and fulfillment. It feels right. You recognize who you are and who you are becoming. Authenticity is all about aligning with the core of your being, your true identity. Your actions, thoughts, words, beliefs, emotions, values, and the image you hold of yourself and your potential reflect this truth of who you are. You act with predictable consistency in your alignment, easing interactions with your consistency. People know they can count on you and are inspired to find the highest within themselves.

Cellular Wisdom at Work

 The dynamic quality of life is so beautifully modeled by the continual turnover of cells, replenishment of the red blood cells every ninety days, remodeling of bone, growth of new blood vessels, birth of neurons in selected regions of the brain, extension of projections of neurons, recovery of function and on and on and on.

Our bodies are never done as long as we are alive. Similarly, the evolution of our Purpose is never complete but opens to more possibilities and dimensions, leading from one dream to another.

Message to the Reader

An individual's Purpose is much larger than a single dream, much larger than could be accomplished in a single lifetime. We don't have to worry about ever completing it, because our Purpose will forever expand as our understanding of it deepens.

> *The exciting part is that we will never get it all done; there will always be something more to which to aspire, and it is in the reaching for an aspiration that we draw more creative energy—life force—through us.*

What is it that motivates a single-cell organism to eventually evolve into a complex, multicellular organism? The single-celled life form has everything it needs to survive. It has the ability to procure food, to digest the food, and to eliminate the leftovers. It can move. It can reproduce. What would cause it to think it could become more? Could it be that Life itself contains the desire to grow and expand its own possibilities, even in its most elementary forms? Is the desire to evolve within the very life force? Does an individual human being share that inner urging with all forms of life? Does this yearning come from our essence ? Is its Purpose to fulfill its highest potential, and we—and our cells—are part of that plan? Is *this* the ultimate wisdom our cells offer us?

This is what will give our lives meaning. This is what will supply the passion. This is what will enable us to connect with aspects of our true essence, to become whole. This is how we will express "the fullness of our being" in the outer world through our work.

This is the essence of what "being authentic" is all about. It is about Living—on Purpose. It is about expressing our unique gifts into the outer world through our work, our relationships, our recreation, our devotion. It is about *being who we are and continually bringing forth more of our greatness.*

We hope your journey of self-discovery will reveal new depths and ways you can express the fullness of Life. We hope you will answer your inner call to be in the fullness of who you truly are and express what that means to you into your outer world through Living on Purpose. We hope you will choose to add your own unique lines to *the new story.*

It's hard for me to believe it has been twelve years since I founded Beyond Success. In many ways I felt like a witness to the unfolding of my dream—to evoke greatness. Often when I hang up the phone or leave a meeting room I am thrilled to be able to contribute to others realizing their dream. The joy has compounded. My gratitude for this work fills me day after day after day. Sometimes before I speak when I look over the many eyes watching me I feel the energy of their drive to find the work that fulfills, to bring more and more of who they are into their work and make a greater and greater contribution to the world. I want to yell at the top of my voice, "Yes, you can! Yes, it *is* possible! I am living proof of it!"

The Top of the Building

It's been a long climb. You started at the sidewalk level and began taking one step at a time, aided a time or two by a serendipitous tip toward an escalator. Any time you tried to skip steps, move faster than the next logical step, you stumbled. But you backed up and took them in order and kept at it. Now, finally, your next step, a final, single step of six or seven inches, will put you at the top of the skyscraper. You take the last step, open the door, and step out onto the flat roof that overlooks an entire city. There is still one more thing you must do, one more task before you are ready to move on to the next dream, the next vision, the next project. This step is one that is almost entirely overlooked in today's hurry-up, more, more, more world. **You see, it is time to pause, to acknowledge your**

accomplishment, to own the achievement, to not only appreciate the small successes, but the big ones, too, to take responsibility for the impact of your dream.

Did you get your dream job or find your dream career? Write that best-selling book? Start a successful business? Create an ideal place for yourself in a larger corporation? Design an innovation that will save people time, money, and effort? Create something of extraordinary beauty? Did you move across the country and reinvent yourself? Did you connect more meaningfully with your core identity? Discover that you are much more than you ever dreamed? Did you get an idea of the scope of your personal Life's Purpose?

Look out across the bustling city. Feel the wind caress your cheeks and the sun warm your shoulders. It is your time to allow yourself to bask for a few moments, hours, or days in the satisfaction of what you have done. This is your reward, your food, and it comes from inside. You could receive an endless number of awards, words of commendation, or recognition, but they will not nourish you. The **nourishment happens internally**. This is the second part of accepting responsibility for your actions and your life. Appreciate the positive impact you have made.

Take a moment to think back to where you were before you began this particular journey. What was your life like? Were you happy? Did you feel filled full? Were you challenged to find the best within you, or were you just getting by? Did you have any energy, any passion, any hope of realizing a dream? Did you know who you are, or were you afraid to ask? What was the logical outcome of your previous trajectory? If you had continued as you were, where would you have ended up?

Now think back over your journey up the staircase. Who did you meet along the way? What friends did you make? What helpers came to your aid with a bottle of water or an encouraging word? What relationships deepened as a result of your climb up the staircase? What opportunities came that you would never have expected? What new skills did you learn? New strategies? For what words did you learn a deeper meaning? What vision helped you keep on course? Remember the times you wanted to give up? What resources did you find inside that kept you going? How is the world a better place because you dared to dream, to Live on Purpose? Who was touched by it? Whose life changed? How is your life different than it was before? How has your trajectory shifted from what it was previously?

You did it. It was *you*, who changed your own life so others could change theirs. *You* were the one who found the courage to leave what was familiar in search of something better. *You* were the one who made a decision to begin to live with determination and volition,

---

You ARE the creation of extraordinary beauty.

Congratulations!

Good job. Well done.

---

choosing the new course of your future.

This is the true joy in life, the being used for a purpose recognized by yourself as a mighty one; the being a force of nature instead of a feverish selfish clod of ailments and grievances complaining that the world will not devote itself to making you happy. I am of the opinion that my life belongs to the whole community and as long as I live it is my privilege to do for it whatever I can. I want to be thoroughly used up when I die, for the harder I work, the more I live. I rejoice in life for its own sake. Life is no 'brief candle' to me. It is sort of a splendid torch which I have a hold of for the moment, and I want to make it burn as brightly as possible before handing it over to future generations. —George Bernard Shaw

Intent into Action
Tools for Chapter 7: Leadership and Living on Purpose

Understanding the nature of the ripple effect, you become more aware of how your personal actions, values, emotions, words, thoughts, and decisions affect the world at large. It makes you aware that what you do actually matters, in the greater scheme of things. It also can inspire you to take a look at the quality of the ripples you are sending out. Aligned ripples sent from a core value of wisdom—making the best use of integrated conscious and unconscious knowledge—are the most powerful ripples you can send! It may take a lifetime to accomplish, but you will never get there if you don't get started. This is the essence of Living on Purpose: pursuing your livelihood from a basis of wisdom, alignment, and ownership of your greatness. It is also the essence of the new story. The dream is only the vehicle you use to express this value, and as a result, you can elect to pursue many dreams if you so desire. Achieving a dream is not nearly as important as who you become in the process of making the pursuit.

As you practice new patterns of thinking and being, others will notice and look to you for leadership. This doesn't necessarily mean you become the CEO or president or owner of an activity. It means that because of how you live your life, others want to emulate you. They recognize something that is perhaps missing in their own life that they wish were there. You don't have to "teach" in order for others to learn from or be touched by your example. All you have to do is practice alignment and wisdom in your daily activities, and others will notice the ripples and learn. And by so doing, you will also be changing your life experience for the better.

Living on Purpose is a beautiful thing. Leadership comes naturally as a result of it. Remember that leading from the inside out is the message of your inner wisdom. It is about how you live your life. It is about the quality of your character. It is about the relationship you have with yourself and your inherent greatness.

This is the process of changing your world, one story at a time. It is how you can reach the top of the building by taking the next step. Even if you change your dream three times or twenty, if you have learned to embrace the magnificence of your own greatness and have abandoned doubt and fear in favor of courage and alignment, you will NOT have failed. From this foundation you will always Live on Purpose.

- *Leadership is about who you are, not what you say or do. It is about practicing a more productive way of doing things and about personally owning the impact you make on your world.*

- *Living on Purpose is about pursuing your livelihood from alignment and wisdom. It is about finding the movement your being has chosen to be in the fullness of who you are and expressing that into the outer world.*

- *When you get to the top of the building, you aren't finished until you pause and celebrate what you have created!*

About the Author

Joan's life experiences include religious training as a Dominican Sister for eleven years in New Orleans, where she first studied and then taught the majority of the college chemistry courses for six years. Leaving the convent, Joan entered graduate school to earn an M.S. in experimental psychology from the University of New Orleans and a Ph.D. in neuroscience and physiological psychology from Tulane University. At Tufts, Joan led a research lab in neuroendocrinology funded by the National Institutes of Health and the National Science Foundation. She taught and directed neuroscience courses for medical, dental and veterinary students for almost twenty years and served as Chair of the Department of Anatomy and Cellular Biology as well as a Director of a Center of Research Excellence serving the three campuses of Tufts (Boston, Medford and Grafton, MA) for five years.

Finding herself at a dynamic crossroad of personal self-discovery, unable to bring all of who she was into the medical world, Joan left academia to found her coaching business. Joan C. King founded her professional coaching business, Beyond Success, LLC, in 1998 after a sabbatical and leave of absence from her duties at Tufts University Schools of Medicine. This time gave Joan permission to stop, examine, and reconstruct her entire life's calling. Today, Joan is an author and international speaker and seminar leader. Joan's formulation and exploration of her "Cellular Wisdom" series of books explores the preverbal wisdom within our cells and its messages. For more information: *http://www .cellular-wisdom.com.*

As one of 600 plus Master Certified Coaches worldwide, today Joan coaches clients, trains coaches in the Success Unlimited Network™ Program, mentors coaches in the Core Passion Coaching Program and the Certified Financial Coach Program, and offers continuing education credits to advanced coaches in her "Coaching from Cellular Wisdom" and her "Mastering Mentoring" Programs. Sought after as an international speaker, Joan's passion is to evoke her greatness and that of everyone she works with. When you hear her speak or read her books, she always asks, "Who are you to deprive the world of your greatness?"

Acknowledgements

Women and men whose awareness penetrates the observable world, who resonate with the unseen harmony that underlies apparent chaos, have always fascinated me. These extraordinary individuals operate from a different level of understanding. They live large. The concepts expressed in Cellular Wisdom emerged during the year and a half in which I re-examined my understanding of neurons from a different perspective. I explored the potential relevance of how cells thrive to our capacity to live large.

I am very thankful to all the readers who volunteered to read and review stages of this book's development. My sincere thanks goes to the following Reader Reviewers: Aleada Branch, Phan Goh, Pepper Makepeace, Joshua McDaniel, Teresa Untiedt, David Quijano, Mary Filapek & Lou Ann Townsend, Victoria Downing, Teresa Espaniola, Carole Balawender, Barbra Espey, Bob Schneider, and Laura Daniel.

Teresa Espaniola's contributions to the cover design and Fleur di Lis Design's contribution to the interior design of the book deserves grateful recognition.

My teachers, both formal and informal, stamped their spirit on this work in fundamental ways; they have stretched and deepened my understanding of the capabilities of the human spirit.

My students and friends ask the questions that lead me to probe the concepts from myriad perspectives and gather the gold hidden in the depths.

I acknowledge the enormous legacy that all of you have graced me with.

Letter to the Reader

Dear Reader,

Many of you who have picked up this book to read have felt alone, isolated, wondering why you are not satisfied with what others are satisifed with—wanting more. You are NOT alone! Many of us have begun the journey to deeper meaning and purpose secretly nurturing our yearnings. You may have berated yourself for wanting more, more purpose, more meaning. Know that your yearning for more will lead you to discover the path to fulfill it. In following your path, you will bring forth more and more of your greatness. In the end, we will all benefit as you bring your contributions to the world. Do not be discouraged. You and your contributions are needed to make our world whole.

I encourage you to find others who are attracted to this book and to read and discuss the book together. You will recognize each other and support each other in this journey to discovering your purpose.

Contact me and I will visit you, in person if possible, by phone, or via Skype.

You are the salt of the earth.

Warm regards,

Joan C. King